BE
FEARLESS

BE
FEARLESS

CHANGE YOUR LIFE
IN 28 DAYS

JONATHAN ALPERT
and
ALISA BOWMAN

**CENTER
STREET**

NEW YORK NASHVILLE

Center Street
Hachette Book Group
1290 Avenue of the Americas, New York, NY 10104
centerstreet.com
twitter.com/centerstreet

Originally published in hardcover and ebook by Center Street in April 2012
First Trade Paperback Edition: January 2019

Center Street is a division of Hachette Book Group, Inc. The Center Street name and logo are trademarks of Hachette Book Group, Inc.

The publisher is not responsible for websites (or their content) that are not owned by the publisher.

The Hachette Speakers Bureau provides a wide range of authors for speaking events. To find out more, go to www.HachetteSpeakersBureau.com or call (866) 376-6591.

Library of Congress Cataloging-in-Publication Data is available

ISBNs: 978-1-5460-8485-3 (trade paperback), 978-1-4555-1339-0 (ebook)

Printed in the United States of America

LSC-C

10 9 8 7 6 5 4 3 2 1

For Mom, with lots of love. Also for Dad, who,
until your passing, taught me how to live a life worthy
of respect. You always were a true gentleman. Even though
you're not with us anymore, your love, wisdom, and
presence live on in me and the many lives you touched.

Contents

Preface to the Trade Edition

In April of 2012, just days before the hardcover version of *Be Fearless* was released, I wrote an Opinion piece for the *New York Times*, titled "In Therapy Forever? Enough Already" (April 22, 2012). The piece shed light on something I had been seeing for years: interminable therapy. In other words, people who remained in therapy, despite not getting better. They felt stuck, mired even. They invested thousands of dollars and, in some cases, felt worse.

The article would be controversial. I knew that, but I hoped to spark a thoughtful conversation and spirited debate about what truly helps people—and what does not. To some extent that happened, but I also received countless hate emails from therapists around the globe. Colleagues attempted to petition the state to get my license revoked. In a vitriol-fueled speech, a New York University commencement speaker warned graduates that I didn't know what I was talking about. My graduate school alma mater, a fine institution that I thought would welcome critical thinking, banned me from an online networking group. Therapists wrote salacious articles about me that were based not on fact but, ironically, fear: the very thing this book is about.

The article was also highly acclaimed by therapists worldwide who believe as I do: Let's try to help patients get better (not just feel better), be self-sufficient, and graduate from therapy. They praised my courage to speak up. Patients who had been stuck in therapy for years, decades even, wrote to tell me how refreshing it was to know that they didn't have to stay in therapy, especially when they were not improving.

Was it worth it, to be a whistleblower of sorts, to call out nearly an entire profession that had been set in its ways for decades? You bet it was. My guess is that Sigmund Freud, the father of analysis, would be disappointed by how his theory evolved after his death and where it has led people: to endless therapy.

I'm encouraged by the continued acceptance of cognitive-behavioral therapy, which forms the basis of the advice in this book and which remains the only empirically based form of therapy. Most of all, I feel confident knowing that, by speaking up and facing such an intense backlash, I did exactly what I recommend in the pages of this book: I faced down my fear. That's how I know you can do the same.

In Therapy Forever? Enough Already[1]

"My therapist called me the wrong name."

"I poured out my heart; my doctor looked at his watch."

"My psychiatrist told me I had to keep seeing him or I would be lost."

New patients tell me things like this all the time. And they tell me how former therapists sat, listened, nodded, and offered little or no advice, for weeks, months, sometimes years. A patient

---

1 Originally published in the *New York Times* April 22, 2012.

recently told me that, after seeing her therapist for several years, she asked if he had any advice for her. The therapist said, "See you next week."

When I started practicing as a therapist fifteen years ago, I thought complaints like this were anomalous. But I have come to a sobering conclusion over the years: that ineffective therapy is disturbingly common.

Talk to friends, keep your ears open at a cafe, or read discussion boards online about length of time in therapy. I bet you'll find many people who have remained in therapy long beyond the time they thought it would take to solve their problems. According to a 2010 study published in the *American Journal of Psychiatry*, 42 percent of people in psychotherapy use 3 to 10 visits for treatment, while 1 in 9 have more than 20 sessions.

For this 11 percent, therapy can become a dead-end relationship. Research shows that, in many cases, the longer therapy lasts the less likely it is to be effective. Still, therapists are often reluctant to admit defeat.

A 2001 study published in the *Journal of Counseling Psychology* found that patients improved most dramatically between their seventh and tenth sessions. Another study, published in 2006 in the *Journal of Consulting and Clinical Psychology*, looked at nearly 2,000 people who underwent counseling for 1 to 12 sessions and found that, while 88 percent improved after one session, the rate fell to 62 percent after 12. Yet, according to research conducted at the University of Pennsylvania, therapists who practice more traditional psychotherapy treat patients for an average of 22 sessions before concluding that progress isn't being made. Just 12 percent of those therapists choose to refer their stagnant patients to another practitioner. The bottom line: Even though extended therapy is not always beneficial, many therapists persist in leading patients on an open-ended, potentially endless, therapeutic course.

Proponents of long-term therapy have argued that severe psychological disorders require years to manage. That may be true, but it's also true that many therapy patients don't suffer severe disorders. Anxiety and depression are the top predicaments for which patients seek mental health treatment; schizophrenia is at the bottom of the list.

In my experience, most people seek therapeutic help for discrete, treatable issues: They are stuck in unfulfilling jobs or relationships, they can't reach their goals, are fearful of change and depressed as a result. It doesn't take years of therapy to get to the bottom of those kinds of problems. For some of my patients, it doesn't even take a whole session.

Therapy can—and should—focus on goals and outcomes, and people should be able to graduate from it. In my practice, the people who spent years in therapy before coming to me were able to face their fears, calm their anxieties, and reach life goals quickly—often within weeks.

Why? I believe it's a matter of approach. Many patients need an aggressive therapist who prods them to face what they find uncomfortable: change. They need a therapist's opinion, advice, and structured action plans. They don't need to talk endlessly about how they feel or about childhood memories. A recent study by the National Institute for Health and Welfare in Finland found that "active, engaging, and extroverted therapists" helped patients more quickly in the short term than "cautious, nonintrusive therapists."

This approach may not be right for every patient, but the results described in the Finnish study are consistent with my experience.

If a patient comes to me and tells me she's been unhappy with her boyfriend for the past year, I don't ask, as some might, "How do you feel about that?" I already know how she feels about that. She just told me: She's unhappy. When she asks me what I think she should do, I don't respond with a return interrogatory, like "What do you think you should do?" If she knew, she wouldn't ask me for my thoughts.

Instead, I ask what might be missing from her relationship and sketch out possible ways to fill in relationship gaps or, perhaps, to end it in a healthy way. Rather than dwell on the past and hash out stories from childhood, I encourage patients to find the courage to confront an adversary, take risks, and embrace change. My aim is to give patients the skills needed to confront their fear of change, rather than to nod my head and ask how they feel.

In graduate school, my classmates and I were taught to serve as guides, whose job it is to help patients reach their own conclusions. This may work, but it can take a long time. I don't think patients want to take years to feel better. They want to do it in weeks or months.

Popular misconceptions reinforce the belief that therapy is about resting on a couch and talking about one's problems. So that's what patients often do. And just as often this leads to codependence. The therapist, of course, depends on the patient for money, and the patient depends on the therapist for emotional support. And, for many therapy patients, it is satisfying just to have someone listen, and they leave sessions feeling better.

But there's a difference between feeling good and changing your life. Feeling accepted and validated by your therapist doesn't push you to reach your goals. To the contrary, it might even encourage you to stay mired in dysfunction. Therapy sessions can work like spa appointments: They can be relaxing but they don't necessarily help solve problems. More than an oasis of kindness or a cozy hour of validation and acceptance, most patients need smart strategies to help them achieve realistic goals.

I'm not against therapy. After all, I practice it. But ask yourself: If your hairstylist keeps giving you bad haircuts, do you keep going back? If a restaurant serves you a lousy meal, do you make another reservation? No, I'm sure you wouldn't, and you shouldn't stay in therapy that isn't helping you, either.

Introduction

Imagine your life one year from now. If it's the same as it is right now, are you okay with that?

I've posed this question to countless clients, friends, and colleagues. Most ponder, shake their heads, and give a firm "No."

I then ask, "What are you doing to change your life?" Most stare blankly and softly mutter, "Nothing."

They feel stuck, as if there's nothing they can do about their futures. They want to change their lives, but they don't know how.

I'm guessing you feel the same. Maybe you are sick of your job, a dysfunctional relationship, or a group of toxic friends or family members. Or perhaps you've always wanted to do something—go back to school, change careers, travel the world, or run a marathon. Or you may have wanted to walk away from a bad habit—to stop smoking, for instance.

It's possible that you've wanted to change your life for some time—for weeks, months, or possibly even years.

But something keeps stopping you.

That something is fear.

Fear is what makes you think that dream of yours is just out of reach. It's what causes you to obsess about that mess in your life—the one that makes you feel out of control, overwhelmed, and dissatisfied—but do nothing about it. It's what keeps you up at night, tossing and turning because you have a vague feeling that your life isn't all it could be. It's what holds you back from advancing in your career, creating fulfilling relationships, and getting what you want in life.

Indeed, fear is the epicenter of all unhappiness. It's what lies behind every problem, and it's what is keeping you stuck.

Think About It

Why do some people stay in jobs or relationships they find unfulfilling? They do it because they are *afraid* they won't be able to find anything better. Why do some people shy away from public speaking and other types of presentations? It's because they are *afraid* people will roll their eyes or laugh at them. Why don't people ask for what they really want? They are *afraid* they won't get it. Think about what you keep putting off in your life. What is the fear that is keeping you stuck?

Because of your fear, you might believe that the following dreams are impossible:

- Reaching the top of your profession
- Starting your own business
- Going back to school to start a new career
- Finding "the one"
- Traveling somewhere you've always wanted to go
- Giving a toast at a wedding
- Overcoming panic, anxiety, depression, or phobias

But all of those dreams—and many more—are possible. They are not out of reach. They only seem impossible because of your fear.

Like you, many of my clients initially thought their dreams were impossible. Then they realized that there was only one thing standing between them and what they really wanted. It wasn't luck. It wasn't a trust fund. And it wasn't circumstance.

It was fear. With my help, they learned how to overcome it. They realized that the difference between the unfulfilled and the fulfilled wasn't the presence or the absence of fear. It was what they did with it. The unfulfilled feel fear and give up. The fulfilled feel it and use it to their advantage. I've worked with countless clients to help them face one fear after another. They have gone on to turn their dreams into reality and live fearless lives.

You can do the same.

You can live a fearless life. You can turn your dreams into reality. You can have all that you want. You can overcome the barriers that are standing between you and success, happiness, and love.

You can create the life that you were meant to live. *Be Fearless* will show you how. All it takes is your willingness to try.

My Promise to You

I wrote this book out of a deep desire to help others. Like you, I was once filled with fear—fear that caused me to get stuck and miss out on what I really wanted out of life. Most of my clients have struggled with fear. We've all been where you are right now.

I also wrote this book out of my frustration with what *didn't* work. Countless clients had told me about the years they'd already spent in therapy—therapy that had only caused them to become more fearful rather than less. It was the same with various books and programs that they had tried. Nothing had worked, and it was a shame. It wasn't their fault. Way too often clients complained about that clichéd line therapists say: "How does that make you feel?" These therapists were using it as a crutch, and it was frustrating. My clients told me they found that one question maddening and even offensive.

They deserved better. With my help, they got better, and they did so quickly. You will do the same.

I want you to know that my approach isn't like that of other therapists or like that of many self-help books. Some of the BE FEARLESS prescriptions are counterintuitive and paradoxical. Quite a few are controversial, too.

But they work.

I've used these paradoxical yet practical prescriptions on countless clients, all of whom have used the five-step BE FEARLESS plan to conquer many types of fears, including fear of failure, fear of rejection, fear of change, fear of public speaking, and even fear of not pleasing their partners in bed. They've found the courage to pursue their passions and become what they've always wanted to become—chefs, teachers, attorneys, doctors, actors, and more. They've been able to get out of dead-end jobs and relationships. They've found true love, and they have become highly successful.

They are creating and living their ultimate lives.

You can emulate them and go on to create your ultimate life too.

Based on the amount of time it has taken my clients to see results, I can assure you that:

- **Within just 24 hours,** you will already be creating the life you want to live.
- **In as soon as 7 days,** you will have broken the fearful patterns that have held you hostage for so long, and you will be feeling triumphant as a result.

- **In approximately 2 weeks,** you will be practicing the art of fearlessness and will already feel more in control and optimistic about your life.
- **In as little as 28 days,** you will have crossed a goal off your "Dream List" and you will have proven the following to yourself: **It's easier to move forward than it is to stay stuck.** You will also realize that your goals are not only worth attempting, they really are possible.

You will achieve success. The BE FEARLESS program will help you to reach the many life goals you've been putting off. You'll learn how your thoughts, beliefs, medications, desire to please others, expectations, self-talk, and even your therapist might be holding you back. You'll rewrite your inner narrative, calm your nerves, and take small but confident steps toward your goal. And you'll become just as fearless and successful as many of my clients have become, and as I have become too.

What Doesn't Work

Why is change so elusive? Why have you been stuck for so long? It's quite possible that you've been looking for a shortcut—a way to get what you want without facing your fear. Perhaps you have resorted to:

Waiting. Rather than being proactive and taking the initiative, perhaps you have spent time hoping that the right person will magically walk into your life, that the job promotion will just materialize, or that your spouse will suddenly start behaving in a less irritating way. If you wait for your dreams to unfold, your dreams will remain just that. If you take action, you'll turn your dreams into a reality. The BE FEARLESS program will help you find the courage to take that initiative.

Wishing. I am not a fan of *The Secret* and the so-called Law of Attraction on which it is based. I can't tell you how many clients came to me after they wished and wished and wished for better lives—only for their lives to continually get worse. The BE FEARLESS program teaches you how to stop wishing and start living.

Blaming. Have you blamed others for your problems? Perhaps you've gotten angry at your boss, your spouse, or someone else for making your life miserable. The BE FEARLESS program will teach you how to stop focusing on what you can't control and, instead, to put your energy into all of the things you can control. You can control what you say and do. It's not as easy to control what other people say and do.

Waiting, wishing, and blaming will not lead you to the life you really want. What will? The BE FEARLESS program.

Five Steps to the Rest of Your Life

The BE FEARLESS program will help you to live to your ultimate potential so you can find true love, happiness, and success. Here's a preview.

Step 1: Define your dream life. To find the passion and motivation you need to face your fear, you'll create your Dream List. On it, you'll write everything you would do if you didn't feel limited by fear (stress, discomfort, the unknown, change, and so on). You will dig deep, get honest with yourself, and define what you truly want. In the roughly three hours it will take you to complete the five simple yet powerful exercises in this step, you will have developed the courage to change your life. You will no longer feel stuck, and your goals and dreams will finally feel within reach.

Step 2: Break your fear pattern. Many people don't realize how they are being limited by fear. In this step you will diagnose, understand, and counter your personal fear pattern, the one that has been keeping you stuck in an unfulfilling life. In the short one to three hours it will take to complete the four short exercises here, you will finally understand what has stood in your way. More important, you'll know how to overcome your barriers to success.

Step 3: Rewrite your inner narrative. You'll complete five exercises over the course of one week that will revolutionize the way you think about change. You'll overcome the negativity and self-doubt that has held you back. You'll develop an inner voice that is positive and encouraging. You'll learn how to become your own greatest fan.

Step 4: Eliminate your fear response. In just two hours, you'll gain the skills you need to deal with nerves, anxiety, worry, stress, and panic. These sensations—racing heart rate, sweaty palms, dry mouth, and clouded thinking—can feel even scarier than your dream. To overcome them, you'll complete six life-changing exercises that will help you to transform fear into a strength.

Step 5: Live your dream. By creating and embarking on a Fearless Action Plan, you will finally change your life and you will do it quickly. You will make one small change at a time, each one leading to the next. In this way you will fearlessly progress toward your goal. Each change will bring you success—success that reinforces your fearlessness and paves the road to happiness.

By following the BE FEARLESS program, you will:

- Find the courage to be who you really are, rather than the person you think others want you to be.
- Overcome the sting of criticism or the need to continually seek approval from others.

- Take strategic action at home, in career, and in relationships so you can reach your true potential.
- Achieve what you once thought impossible, such as confront a spouse or coworker, network with grace, deliver a presentation, build a career you love, or be yourself on a date.
- Gain a sense of control amid seemingly uncontrollable situations that range from job loss to romantic disappointments.

You will feel complete, and you will have cleaned up the mess that has been keeping you up at night. You will go to bed happy, you will sleep soundly, and you will wake up ready to fearlessly face the day.

Change Your Life Now!

The BE FEARLESS program will help you to overcome fear of change, failure, criticism, and more, and it will help you to do it in just 28 days. You really can land your dream job, find love, and create a fulfilling life, but it will take a commitment. Get your calendar. On it set the following deadlines:

One week from today: Finish reading this book.

Two weeks from today: Embark on the BE FEARLESS five-step program.

Three weeks from today: Continue to move fluidly through the steps and have Step 5 within sight.

Four weeks from today: Create your Fearless Action Plan and embark on your first of many life changes.

BE
FEARLESS

PART ONE

Prepare to
BE FEARLESS

Chapter One

How I Became Fearless—and How You Will Too!

You've probably tried to overcome your fear and do something about your problems. Maybe you've spent months sitting on a therapist's couch. Or perhaps you are no stranger to the self-help section of the bookstore. Yet nothing seems to work.

Why am I so confident that I have the winning formula that will help you change your life when other experts, books, and programs have already failed you? I'm confident because the BE FEARLESS five-step plan grew out of my personal experience. You see, I might seem fearless now, but I haven't always been this way.

Like you I was once held back by my fear, and I missed out on life because I was too scared to take a chance. By overcoming my own fears, I was able to become a highly competent therapist and better understand my fearful clients. I know, for instance, exactly why my clients struggle with change and uncertainty because I've struggled with change and uncertainty too. I am able to draw from what I've learned in overcoming my own fear so I can lead my clients to the same fearless place I've already found for myself.

Some of my clients spent years mired in therapy before coming to see me. They tried to change their lives so many times. Many told me, during the first appointment, that they had little hope. They doubted I could help them. You can probably imagine how gratifying it was for me to watch them conquer their fears and change their lives so quickly. Usually by the end of that very first appointment, they were already feeling more positive. For most, it took only a few appointments—less than a month—before they found the courage to make the first of several changes in their lives. Nearly all of them—no matter how lofty their dreams or seemingly impossible their goals—graduated from therapy in just a few months.

Their goals and fears differed, but the process for changing their lives did not. I soon realized that my clients were able to face their fears and change their lives by progressing through the same five steps. Those steps have become the BE FEARLESS program.

I'd like to tell you the story of how I used my fear to help others. It's my hope that by sharing this story, you will be able to see that a similar transformation is just as possible for you.

The Girl I Never Kissed

My fearful-to-fearless story starts in early childhood. As a toddler I wore Forrest Gump leg braces. In elementary school I spoke funny, couldn't pronounce certain words, and had to attend speech class. Until seventh grade I was at least several inches taller than my classmates.

Through my high school years I was terribly shy and so fearful of attention that I avoided parties, dances, football games, and social gatherings. While my classmates were at the prom, I was by myself, aimlessly driving my parents' Oldsmobile station wagon—yes, the kind with the fake wood siding.

I was especially fearful of girls. In my mind, they were big, bad monsters. They would never go for a tall, skinny, awkward boy like me. They would laugh at me. I was sure of it. Still, there was this one girl I really liked. Her name was Katie. She was popular, had lots of friends, and sat next to me in class, but only because our last names both started with the letter A.

I'm embarrassed to admit that to get Katie's attention, I tried all sorts of dysfunctional and ineffective tactics. Yes, I was one of those suckers who, out of desperation, fell for an advertisement in the back of a magazine for a pheromone spray called "Attractant 10." The spray was supposed to render me "irresistible to women." Interestingly, the product is still around today.

I ordered and began using the product right away. I put it on just before class. Yet Katie seemed unaffected. One day I managed to time things so that we walked out of school at the same moment. Here she was, right next to me! We were walking in the same direction. No one else was around. It was just us.

I managed to mutter an awkward hello and chat a little bit. Then she turned to go in another direction. It was now or never. If I was going to ask her out, this was my only chance.

"See you tomorrow," she said.

"Yeah, see you," I said.

She walked away. I'd blown it.

I was eighteen years old before I was brave enough to even kiss someone and well into my twenties before I dated regularly. I eventually overcame my fear, however, and developed the courage to ask women out with confidence. I went on to face and overcome many other fears, ranging from fear of failure to fear of criticism. Each time I faced my fear, I realized I emerged stronger and more confident. Over time, I began to see that fear was not something to hide from. It wasn't a reason to abandon my goals or dreams either. It was merely a temporary stressor. If I pushed through the short-term stress, I was able to move past the fear and get to any long-term goal I set for myself. This realization helped me to get through graduate school, develop my own practice, and deliver a style of therapy that is highly effective, innovative, and even gutsy at times.

BE FEARLESS: *Change is scary and often causes temporary stress. That's why our natural reaction is to withdraw and hide. Yet this short-term stress is worth the long-term gain of greater happiness and peace of mind.*

Daring to Be Me

I became a psychotherapist because I've always been fascinated with human behavior and psychology. Even as a shy kid, I gravitated toward people who had been ostracized because of their psychological challenges. Later, as a teen, I had a date with the famed sex therapist Dr. Ruth Westheimer every Sunday night, when I listened to her radio show on my Sony Walkman when I probably should have been sleeping. I not only learned from her, I aspired to eventually grow up and become the male version of her. I wanted to be in a career that allowed me to help people and make a difference, and I wanted to reach the masses. Like Dr. Ruth, I wanted to use the media as a tool to help hundreds and even thousands of other people. I wanted to help people overcome their psychological challenges and go on to achieve greatness, and I wanted to do this in a big way.

Soon after I became a psychotherapist, however, I realized that I could not be the type of psychotherapist my schooling had trained me to become. In graduate school, I had been taught to help clients come to realizations by simply asking insightful questions. My schooling had warned against injecting my opinion into a therapy session. Rather than telling clients what to do, I was supposed to sit, listen, and ask what has now become a clichéd and frustrating question: "How does that make you feel?"

I just couldn't do it.

Rather than simply listening as clients vented, I found myself continually injecting my opinion, offering advice, and creating structured action plans for them.

For instance, one of my early clients came to me because he was living a lie and as a result was depressed. I'll call him Rick. Rick was married, and he was going to porn shops and having indiscriminate sex with other men.

As I listened to him tell me about his escapades, I kept thinking about his poor wife back at home. Not only was he exposing himself and her to sexually transmitted diseases, he was also forcing her to live a lie. He was a closeted homosexual who was masquerading as a happily married man. I imagined that she probably felt inadequate in the bedroom, wondering why she could not please her husband and why he didn't seem attracted to her.

How could I not say something to Rick? How could I just nod my head and listen as he told me about his infidelity? How could I just sit back and ask, "How does that make you feel?"

I couldn't.

I flat out told him, "This is wrong. It's disgusting." He was shocked. He said, "I've been to eight other therapists and not one of them has ever told me that it was wrong." Rick initially was annoyed with my honesty, but he ended up coming back to see me. He attempted to curb his porn shop visits and sex with strangers while he worked on finding the courage to come out of the closet and develop a healthy sexual relationship.

But his revelation about his previous therapists angered and frustrated me. Eight different therapists had all sat, listened, and said nothing as Rick had told them about what he was doing?

And he wasn't the only one.

I counseled additional clients who told me about past therapists who had dozed off during sessions or called them by the wrong name. They complained, at times, that they felt as if they had been helping their therapists more than their therapists had been helping them. *How does that make you feel?* was a phrase they made fun of. It was generic and it was useless. They admitted to spinning their wheels for years and not getting anywhere.

One of them had been in therapy for a decade! She had gone week after week and paid bill after bill *even though she wasn't getting better.* I asked her, "What were you gaining from these therapy sessions?" She looked at me and answered, "Good question."

I was disgusted with my profession, and I could see that the listening-only approach just wasn't helping people to get better. It only frustrated people. They would come to me and complain, "I've been to a dozen therapists. They just sat there and listened and didn't tell me what to do. I hope you'll be different." I soon found myself constantly explaining that I was not "one of *those* therapists."

BE FEARLESS: *You overcome fear not by avoiding it, but by facing it. The more you face your fear, the more fearless you will become.*

I thought back to the lessons I'd learned from my parents. My parents had taught me to give it my best and always do a good job. They were hardworking and often held second jobs. They encouraged me to work and, from a young age, I did. I delivered newspapers, tended to the locker room at a health club, and even worked as a cleaning person at a motel. They'd said over and over again, "If people are paying you, you give them what they came for. Give them what they need." With that in mind, I knew I wanted to deliver the best service possible, and I would.

Nodding my head and listening was not delivering that service. People were coming to me because they wanted to get better and they wanted to be told how to do that. I eventually decided to abandon the established norms of my field and I set out to help people get better the way I knew how: giving advice.

Therapy in the Real World

Not only did I decide to give advice and tell people what to do, I also decided to counsel them in the real world—in the very places where they felt fearful. Rather than keep them on a couch indoors where they felt safe and did not have to test their limits, I began taking socially anxious people to the park and asking them to walk up and introduce themselves to strangers. I accompanied clients with a fear of heights to rooftops and those who were afraid of elevators to elevators. I met them at their fear.

I told clients that we'd spend a session or two in the office, but most of our therapy would take place in parks, shopping centers, cafés, rooftops, and other locations. "This will allow you to practice important skills," I said. "Therapy in an office is safe. There's the comfortable couch, the quiet room. But will that allow you to face what causes you so much anxiety? You can work on your problems in the real world where they actually occur."

To my delight, nearly all of my potential clients were willing to try this new approach. David was one of them.

Think About It

Facing your fear might feel nearly impossible to you right now. You might think that it's daunting. I understand that. I know that impossible feeling because I've felt it too. So have many of my clients. That's why I'm going to ask you to think about a question:

If I gave you a million dollars, could you find a way to overcome your fear?

I think you could. BE FEARLESS will get you there.

Fear of Approaching the Opposite Sex

David told me that he wanted to overcome shyness and anxiety, so I suggested that we meet at Central Park.

We sat together on a bench. I learned that David was a successful lawyer, but he was terrible with the ladies. If a woman looked at him, he would withdraw and look the other way. He was in his thirties, and he had convinced himself that he'd be living in his Manhattan apartment alone forever.

I couldn't help but notice that David suffered from a similar fear that I'd once had so many years before.

BE FEARLESS: *Being fearless isn't something that some people are born with, and it's not found in a magical pill either. What separates the fearless from the fearful isn't the absence or the presence of fear. Rather, it's what they do with it.*

I asked David to tell me more about his anxiety: when it occurred, what triggered it, how long he'd had it, what he'd already tried to deal with it, and what thoughts led to it. Much like me, David had suffered from anxiety and shyness since his teenage years. Social situations triggered a panic response. Simply going into a bar led to heavy breathing, heart palpitations, and rigidity. Some of this fear had been brought on by social failures. For instance, he'd read some books on how to score with the ladies. Then he'd embarrassed himself by using some really cheesy lines from these books on women he'd met at bars. They'd laughed in his face.

This handsome, educated, and successful guy thought of himself as an unattractive failure. He focused on any minor perceived flaw and magnified it to the point where he had nothing positive to think or say about himself.

I gave him some homework. It was simple. I asked him to come back to the park, get comfortable, and hang out. I suggested that he might read a book, observe people, or listen to music. I taught him a few relaxation exercises, and I asked him to do them before and during his time at the park.

During our next session we walked around the park. I asked him to smile at people and make eye contact. Once he got used to that, we progressed. I asked him to approach strangers and ask them for the time.

"Just watch me," I said. I approached someone, said hello, and asked directions.

"Now you try it," I suggested.

I wanted David to experience something that would provide reassurance. A smile or a look from someone would tell him that he was okay. This would help to replace the negative memory he had of being laughed at when he'd used those pickup lines.

He tried it first with men and then with women, but purposely no one he was attracted to.

Once he was comfortable asking anyone for the time or for directions, I knew he was ready for a bigger challenge: a café.

I took him to a small coffee shop where tables were close together and we could easily hear what our neighbors were talking about and see what they were reading. Again, I asked him to watch and observe as I engaged the stranger next to me in small talk. Then I encouraged him to chime in. He did.

After a while I excused myself to use the bathroom. I didn't really need to use it. I just wanted to give him an opportunity to be alone. On my way back to the table, I saw him chatting with the cute waitress. When I sat down, he told me that she was pursuing a career in acting. In fewer than four minutes he had been able to learn about her career pursuits and hobbies. He had a twinkle of confidence in his eyes and an eagerness to get out there and put his newfound confidence to good use. At that point I knew my man was well on his way to success.

David eventually met someone and developed a relationship. I got a call from him a few weeks later. He explained that he was throwing out his *How to Score with the Ladies* self-help books for two reasons. One, he no longer needed them. Two, his new girlfriend was planning on coming over for a romantic dinner and he didn't want to run the risk of her seeing such books.

I knew he no longer needed my services. David had graduated from therapy, and I was happy for him.

Fear Is Necessary

It's now been several years since I counseled David. I've seen countless numbers of fearful clients. They feared heights, subways, elevators, commitment, love, success, rejection, public speaking, and more. What makes their stories amazing isn't that they were born with a natural confidence. No, what makes them amazing is that they all were quite the opposite. As I once was, as David once was, and as you may be right now, these clients were once almost completely incapacitated by their fear.

I've taught all of them that fear is a tool to be used to their advantage. It's not a sign to run and hide. Rather it's a sign to move forward. Irrational fears—fears of things that can't physically harm us—must be faced.

It's rewarding to see how much progress my clients make from one appointment to the next. I get great satisfaction from knowing that someone is moving toward his or her goals. When clients are no longer held hostage by fear, I ask, "How does it feel to be fearless?"

They always answer that question with a glimmer in their eyes. There's nothing more satisfying for me than to be there with them as they celebrate reaching their goals.

I look forward to the day that you get to the same place. In less than one week, you will be well on your way to conquering the fear that until now has held you back and kept you stuck. In as few as 28 days, you will have completed the BE FEARLESS five-step program, and you will have proven to yourself that fear is a necessary part of success and happiness.

I am thrilled that you've found the courage to take this journey. My only regret is that I will not be able to see the glimmer in your eyes when you realize that you are well on your way to becoming fearless. I know that massive change is possible for you because I've seen it in myself and I've seen it in countless clients.

I can't wait until you can see it in yourself. I'm optimistic about your chances. You can overcome your fear. Yes, you can! It really is possible. Keep reading to find out how.

Change Your Life Now!

Fearlessness is a skill, one that you can acquire and strengthen with a smart, thoughtful strategy, devotion, and motivation. The BE FEARLESS program teaches you the same skills that I've used to overcome my own fear and have used to help countless clients do the same. It's natural to want to avoid fear, but avoidance will only keep you stuck. With the help of the advice in this book, you are going to face your fear. Rather than hide from it, you will move past it. You will face it, overcome it, and, as a result, feel a great sense of triumph. To weaken the hold fear has on you, do the following.

Think of what you are missing because of your fear. What would you love to do if only you weren't so scared? What have you missed out on in life because you've allowed fear to stand in your way? What have you passed up because of fear?

Make a Regret List. On it list all of the things you would have already done with your life if fear were not an obstacle. Carry this list with you and read it over when you have a spare moment. Use it to motivate yourself toward change.

Chapter Two

Why Everyone Fears Change

You are not alone in your fear. I have acquaintances who are afraid of not being able to pay the rent. I know someone who worries she'll never meet the right guy or be able to have a family. Someone else I know fears his earnings will go down for the year. I even know one guy who, at first, seems like a true thrill seeker. He finds things like skydiving and off-road motorcycle riding fun. Do you want to know what brings him to his knees? Snakes!

Fear is ubiquitous. Everyone feels it.

Not only does everyone experience fear, they also feel it for the same reason. All fear shares the same origin: the unknown. Every fear you can think of or name—ranging from fear of success to fear of public speaking—is really about uncertainty. It's about not knowing what will happen next. Will the audience listen with rapt attention or will they fall asleep? Will the snake stay where it is or will it try to bite you? Will your boss give you the promotion you seek or will he demote you instead?

The more uncertain your future, the more you will have to

fear. The more predictable your future, the less you will fear. Until now, this uncertainty has stood between you and the change you seek. It's worked to unravel your motivation and keep you stuck.

The BE FEARLESS program helps you overcome this roadblock to your success by creating certainty in the midst of uncertainty. It starts with visualizing the future you want and ends with creating the future that you imagined. All along the way, you'll work to overcome the genetic wiring that, until now, has worked against you—causing you to expect the worst and doubt the possibility of the best. By overcoming your negativity and creating a realistic action plan, you'll be able to face your fear of the unknown and finally get on with your life.

To help you better understand how it all works, I'd like to tell you a personal story about the fear of the unknown.

The Fear of an Uncertain Future

Several years ago I was driving from New York City to my hometown in Connecticut to visit Mom and Dad for a relaxing weekend. As I always do when I drive, I was listening to music and enjoying the open road. I was just exiting the highway not far from my destination when my phone rang. I pushed the hands-free speaker button and heard that it was Mom calling. Her voice didn't sound right. It was strained.

"Jonathan, it's not good. The report says there are lesions on Dad's brain."

"What do you mean?" I asked, hoping that I'd heard her wrong.

I knew that Dad had been suffering strange symptoms for a few days. It had started after he'd had some dental work. He had tingling sensations and numbness on the left side of his face. He'd thought that the dental work had inflicted some nerve damage, but the dentist had explained that the dental work couldn't have caused such a sensation.

That Friday, as I'd been driving the first of two hours from New York City to Connecticut, my dad had been at the doctor's office learning the results of a recent MRI.

"The doctor told him that he has lesions consistent with metastatic disease," Mom said. "When Dad asked the doctor what that meant, the doctor told us, 'It's not good.' They want to run some more tests. We have to wait and see the results, but it doesn't look good, Jonathan, it doesn't look good."

I could tell that she was trying to be strong and hold it together for my benefit. I was shocked, deeply saddened, and had a million questions running through my mind: *What does this mean? What are the treatment options? How can this be?*

I told Mom that I was just a few miles from home. "I'll be there soon," I said. I nervously drove as quickly as I could, my mind already at my destination.

I walked through the door and hugged my mother. My dad, always so dedicated and hardworking, had already gone back to work. Later, when he arrived home, Dad made spaghetti for all of us. At some point that evening, Mom and I went on the Internet to find out more about what this report meant. The Internet only fueled our fear and anxiety. *Could he really have such an advanced stage of cancer that it had metastasized to his brain?* The more we searched the Internet, the more devastated we felt and the graver the prognosis seemed.

The weekend proved to be the longest weekend of my life, my parents' lives, and the lives of my siblings. The image of my parents embracing and crying is so strong. They'd been married for thirty-eight years and had been together for more than forty. They were inseparable. They truly were the rock of our family.

There is no way this can be happening, I thought.

One town over, my sister, Susan, was feeling a similar disbelief and numbness. "How could it be cancer if he has no symptoms?" she questioned. To soothe herself, she began cleaning. She scrubbed the inside of the fridge and the toaster, and she got the cobwebs out of the corners.

In Washington, D.C., my brother, Matthew, was also in disbelief.

Two agonizingly long days later, it was time for me to head back to New York City. I'll never forget hugging my parents as I left them. The hug lasted a lot longer than it usually does and was much closer. There were tears and with that, I departed, frightened of what might lie ahead.

Dad went back to his doctor the following week. He underwent a PET scan, which provides a much more detailed picture of the inside of the body than an MRI does. Whereas an MRI shows a three-dimensional picture of the inside of the body, a PET scan also reveals the molecular and metabolic function of cells—allowing physicians to determine whether those cells are normal or abnormal (cancerous).

On the day that Dad was meeting with the doctor to review the results, I was back in New York seeing a client. As hard as I tried, I couldn't concentrate on what the client was telling me, and I was going through the motions. Thankfully the client never seemed to notice.

After that appointment, I went to Central Park and just kept walking and walking. So many questions were running through my mind. *What if Dad dies? How will Mom cope? How will I cope? Is this really happening? Is it really terminal cancer? What will we all do?*

Finally, the test was done and Dad got the results. Amazingly, the PET scan revealed no cancer. The lesions were definitely there, but they did not look like cancer. They looked like something else. Dad's doctor said more tests were needed. He wasn't sure if

Dad's lesions were caused by a stroke, high blood pressure, or a neurological disorder like multiple sclerosis (MS).

Dad then was sent to a neurologist who looked at the scans and other test results.

Although some tests were inconclusive, the doctors eventually settled on multiple sclerosis as a diagnosis. In a weird way, the diagnosis came with such relief. I remember thinking, *Thankfully it's not advanced cancer! The lesions are* only *due to the MS!*

It's been several years and my dad is healthy and remains active.

I told you the story of my dad's misdiagnosis to illustrate a point: we fear what we don't know. That long weekend, we were, of course, afraid of cancer, but behind that was a fear of the unknown. We didn't know if Dad was going to be okay or if he wasn't going to be okay. If Dad wasn't going to be okay, we didn't know how we would all hold up. Would I, for instance, be able to be there for him and still be able to manage my therapy practice two hours away in New York? Was I strong enough emotionally to watch my father get sick and possibly die? Was my mother? How would my mom do things that she relied so heavily on Dad to do? Would she be okay without him?

And even the so-called cancer was unpredictable because we didn't have enough information. Mom and I had attempted to find information on the Internet that would provide us with some predictability and control. We'd craved certainty. We wanted to know what kind of cancer it was, how it would likely progress, and what would eventually happen. We wanted to know what to expect—good or bad.

Once Dad got a definitive diagnosis, the fear subsided. That was because the future was now predictable again. Sure, Dad had MS, but he now knew what to expect and what to do about it. He had a sense of how it would progress, what treatments were available, and where he was going to go from here. The unknowns were replaced with knowns.

It's the same with any fear.

BE FEARLESS: *Focus on what you have control over, not on what's beyond it.*

You Fear What You Don't Know

You might think that the fear you are struggling with right now—the very fear that led to you buying and reading this book—is different from the fear I felt that weekend as I waited for Dad's diagnosis, but it's not different at all.

All fear—ranging from the fear of being bad in bed to the fear of speaking in front of a crowd—is about uncertainty. It comes from an inability to predict the future. I'm guessing that you might be thinking something along the lines of, *How could a fear of snakes possibly be about uncertainty? I fear a snake because it might bite me and kill me. There's nothing uncertain about that.*

Not so fast. Fear of snakes is as much about the unknown as fear of an impending health problem. Here's why. If you are near a snake, you have many unanswered questions. *Is it poisonous? Will I die if I get bitten? If I get bitten and it's poisonous, will I be able to get help? Will anyone even know what to do?*

Now if you were the person in charge of reptiles and amphibians at the local zoo, you might not have a fear of snakes because you would be able to answer such questions. You would know which snakes are poisonous and which ones are not. You would know how to handle a snake so it couldn't bite you. And you would know what to do on the off chance you did get bitten. You would also know that everyone around you was trained in how to deal with snakebites. You wouldn't be fearful because you would have very little if any uncertainty.

It's for this reason that most people are not fearful of mosquitoes and bees. Sure they are nuisances and we avoid them, but they don't generate a panic response. You've probably been bitten by either or both numerous times. You know exactly what will happen if you are bitten, and you know what to do about it too. You put ice or baking soda or an ointment on it and you're done with it. There's no uncertainty, so you are not fearful.

To further convince you, I created the chart that follows. In it, I tried to anticipate a number of fears that you may think have nothing to do with uncertainty.

Fear	How It Relates to Uncertainty
Fear of ending a dead-end relationship	You're uncertain about whether being alone is really better (or possibly worse) than being in a dead-end relationship. You are uncertain about whether you have what it takes to be alone. You are uncertain that you will ever meet anyone else. What if this dead-end relationship is as good as it gets?
Fear of saying yes to a marriage proposal	You're uncertain whether you can really live the rest of your life with this person. You don't know if you have what it takes to be monogamous for life. You are uncertain about whether you will miss your freedom. You feel uncertain about what the future together holds and whether that future is really better than a future alone.

continued

Fear	*How It Relates to Uncertainty*
Fear of excelling at work and climbing the corporate ladder	You're uncertain whether you have what it takes to climb to the next level and continue to excel. You are uncertain whether more responsibility would really make you happier. What if you end up hating it? You are uncertain whether it's better to stay in a boring but easy position than it is to pursue a higher-paying, more interesting position that is also more challenging.
Fear of public speaking	You are uncertain about how the crowd will react to what you have to say. Will they heckle you? Will they walk out? Will they fall asleep? You are uncertain about how others will view you and think of you.
Fear of heights	You are uncertain of your footing and don't know if you can remain steady enough to prevent yourself from falling over an edge.
Fear of flying	You are uncertain about whether the plane will really stay in the sky. You are uncertain about what will transpire between point A and point B. Will there be delays? Will there be lots of turbulence? What will happen if it's really bumpy? Will you get sick? And if you get sick, how will other passengers react?
Fear of not pleasing your partner in bed	You are uncertain about your relationship and whether it is strong enough to withstand your partner not having an orgasm. Will your partner leave you if you are not a rock star in the bedroom?

Fear	How It Relates to Uncertainty
Fear of investing in a business venture	You don't know if it will work out. Will you go broke? Will you make money? Will you be able to pay the mortgage? Or will you lose your house?

Even serious mental health disorders are about uncertainty. Panic disorder, for instance, is characterized by sudden feelings of terror that strike repeatedly and without warning. It relates to uncertainty because of all the unknowns: *When will it strike? Will I be at work when I have a panic attack? If so, what will my coworkers think of me? Will I be driving when I have one? If so, will I be able to control the car? Will I be alone when one hits? If so, what if no one is around to help me?*

Obsessive-compulsive disorder involves repeated, intrusive, and unwanted thoughts or rituals that seem impossible to control. How does it relate to uncertainty? These are the kinds of thoughts someone with OCD has: *Is the door locked? Will there be intruders? Is the door locked?* Or the thoughts might go like this: *Did I touch something that's contaminated? I have to wash my hands. Did I touch something toxic? Then I have to wash my hands.* Those thoughts are all based on uncertainty.

Similarly, in posttraumatic stress disorder—which involves persistent symptoms that occur after experiencing a traumatic event, such as war, rape, child abuse, a natural disaster, or being taken hostage—the fearful thoughts are also based on uncertainty. Someone with PTSD might think any of the following: *Will the stressful event happen again? Will I get raped again? Will I end up in war again? Will the flashback occur again? Will I have to relive this again?*

And finally even when you wake in the middle of the night with free-floating anxiety, it's still about uncertainty. You might be unable to sleep because you are uncertain about work, with thoughts like, *How will I do what I need to do? Am I going to get fired? Will I get done what I need to get done?* You might even be uncertain about getting back to sleep, thinking thoughts like, *What will happen if I toss and turn all night long? Will I be wiped out at work tomorrow? If I'm wiped out at work tomorrow, then what?*

The BE FEARLESS program helps you to overcome this uncertainty by helping you to map out your future. The five exercises in Step 1 will take you less than three hours to complete, but their effects will be long-lasting. By visualizing a dream and testing it out, you will be able to eliminate much of the uncertainty that surrounds change.

The BE FEARLESS program will give you the certainty that you seek, and that certainty will take you anywhere you want to go. But the program goes even further than that. It also helps you to rewrite the negative narrative that plays in your mind, the one that until now has worked to talk you out of attempting to change your life.

Let's take a closer look at why this is so important.

Think About It

Take a moment and think about your own fears. Think about how they might relate to uncertainty. What don't you know about the future? What can't you predict? What are the unknowns, and how do these unknowns add to your anxiety?

Negativity Creates Fear

Your brain prefers predictability, certainty, and control. When things are uncertain and you don't know what's going to happen next, your brain attempts to make up an ending. It writes its own narrative. There are two problems with this narrative. One, it's often not accurate. Two, the narrative is usually negative, and it's these negative thoughts that lead to catastrophic, worst-case-scenario, devastating thinking.

This thinking sounds like this:

- "She'll never like a guy like me."
- "People will think I'm stupid and boring."
- "The bridge is going to collapse."
- "I'll never be a success."
- "I'll never find someone."
- "I'll be alone forever."
- "The jet will crash."

Do you see the common theme in all of those statements? They are all negative predictions. This is known as "the negativity bias." We tend to notice and remember negative events and information over those that are positive. For instance, for most people unhappy memories from their childhoods are often stronger than happy ones. This phenomenon, in part, keeps people like me in business! In marriages, many people will also remember bad times—horrendous fights they've gotten into, for instance—over good times. And most people can rattle off dozens of negative stories about work, but only a few positive stories.

The negativity bias doesn't affect only what we remember from the past. It also affects how we see the future. Because of the negativity bias, we tend to predict doom, gloom, mayhem, and failure. And this leads to fear, making us feel stuck.

Test It Out

Imagine a crosswalk on a busy city street. At one end of the crosswalk, you see a nice young man offering to help a fragile old lady. Across the street, you see a not-so-nice young man arguing with his mother. Which man catches your attention? Which man do you remember? Which man do you go home and tell your family about? Which man stays with you and haunts you? It's the thankless, argumentative son right? That's because of the negativity bias.

This negativity bias has been programmed into our wiring. We can't even blame it on our mothers. We have to go back thousands of years. Back then outcomes generally *were* negative. Many babies died of illness. Most humans met untimely deaths. Wild animals were lurking around most corners.

It made sense to predict negative outcomes because they happened to be the most likely outcomes way back then. Thousands of years ago, early humans who panicked over a loud sound were the early humans who lived to see another day. The negativity bias led to survival.

In modern times, however, the negativity bias is a hindrance, one that reinforces our fear to the point where it becomes debilitating. Until now, you've been a victim of your negativity bias. It has ruled your thoughts and your actions. The BE FEARLESS program will help you to override this bias. The program teaches you to examine and replace habitual negative thinking. You'll test out your negative predictions, come up with more likely scenarios, and write a new, happier, and more realistic ending. In doing so, you'll be better able to make the positive ending come true.

How You'll Overcome Past Failures

Sometimes the negativity bias develops from a real-life negative event, called a *negative reference experience*. For instance, a close friend named Alison has taken hundreds of flights that were all completely uneventful. Then not long ago she was on a plane that experienced a fuel leak and had to make an emergency landing. It was a scary experience. Now whenever she flies, she thinks of that emergency landing! It was just one flight out of hundreds, but that's the flight that comes to mind.

I had a similar experience many years ago, only instead of an airplane it involved a poodle. Yes, a poodle. When I was six years old I was walking with my dad. It was a casual stroll on the weekend, and as we got close to home I did what most rambunctious six-year-olds do: I ran ahead of my dad and around the corner. I was at that age where I was exercising my autonomy. That was all normal and great, but then a minute or two later my dad remembers seeing me running furiously back toward him as a little poodle chased me. It's a funny story that my dad gets a kick out of, especially today. He of course likes to tell the story a little differently, fibbing and saying that I was really sixteen when it took place. It all makes for a good laugh. Yet that one negative experience impacted me for many of my formative years, causing me to feel uncomfortable around dogs.

Negative reference experiences can also be handed down to us from our parents. Many parents teach their children to be fearful of strangers and busy streets, which is a good thing, but many other fears are also learned from watching our parents. My friend

Heather, for instance, has a fear of heights. So does her mother. For many years Heather wasn't sure if she'd learned this fear from her mother or if the two simply shared a genetically induced fear of heights. She got her answer when she had a daughter of her own, a child who initially seemed to be quite fearless.

Eventually her daughter became fearful of heights too, and Heather realized that her daughter was picking up on her own anxiety. Whenever her daughter would attempt to climb up a ladder, Heather would tell her, "No, please don't do that right now." Sometimes if her daughter was doing something perfectly reasonable, such as walking up and down steep steps, Heather would get tense and loudly gasp, and her daughter picked up on it. This now serves as a cue that makes her daughter fearful.

You may or may not be able to remember your negative reference experience. Perhaps the reference experience took place when you were too young to remember it. Or maybe the conditioning that made you fearful was so subtle that you didn't notice it or remember it. That's okay. It's not as important for you to know why you are fearful as it is for you to know what to do about it. Knowing where you want to go is much more important than knowing where you've been. Many people find themselves stuck in therapy for years and years talking about where they were thirty years ago, and they never get out of that stage. I don't believe in keeping you stuck in the past. I want you to learn how to live in the now.

In this book, you'll find out how to move forward. The BE FEARLESS program shows you how to overcome negative reference experiences by testing out the negative predictions they lead to and proving those negative predictions wrong. In this way, you will collect evidence to the contrary and eventually overwrite the negative narrative and replace it with a positive one.

> ### Think About It
>
> Are you getting a sense of why you are fearful? Can you now put two and two together? Can you trace your fear back to a specific reference experience? Can you see how that experience shaped and strengthened your fear?

Why We Feel Nerves

In addition to helping you to overcome the negativity bias, the BE FEARLESS program helps you to deal with sensations of fear. Not only does the program help you to calm your nerves, it even will show you how to use such symptoms as a racing heartbeat to your advantage.

Despite popular belief, nervous sensations are actually quite useful. They date back thousands of years to a time when most of what humans didn't know, didn't understand, or couldn't predict could literally get them killed. If early humans were fearless enough to walk onto an unfamiliar grassy prairie, for instance, they ended up becoming dinner for a wild animal lurking in that grass. So humans and other animals developed a built-in fear of the unknown. In a dangerous, uncertain world, it was quite helpful for early humans to be able to react to danger quickly and effectively. Thus the "fight or flight" response was wired into the nervous system. For the purposes of this book I will, from here on out, refer to this response as your *fear response*.

This fear response is designed to give you a great deal of strength, smarts, and speed when you are under attack. When early humans were confronted by dangerous wild animals, their fear response helped them to run and hide. It also helped them to find the strength needed to club an animal over the head. It even helped them to play dead, if needed.

We rarely confront wild animals in modern times, but the fear response remains. When you are startled, nervous, or stressed, your brain turns on your sympathetic nervous system. This triggers the release of stress hormones such as adrenaline and norepinephrine. From here a cascade of reactions result. These include:

- **Increased energy and strength.** Your heart rate and breathing rate speed up in an effort to provide more oxygenated blood to your muscles. It pumps sugar into your bloodstream so your brain and muscles can burn it easily and quickly, allowing you to run away from or fend off an attacker. This surge of energy and strength has, for instance, allowed mothers to lift cars off their trapped children.
- **Sharper vision and hearing.** This allows you to see and hear better so you can more easily spot dangerous predators.
- **More endurance.** During the fear response, the body sweats. This serves as a precooling mechanism so you are better able to run without getting overheated.
- **Less pain.** During the fear response, the body turns down your perception of pain. It's for this reason that a gunshot victim might not realize he or she has been shot. The pain eventually does kick in—and in a big way—but not until the injured person has gotten to safety and the fear response has subsided.

When your fear response is flipped on, your entire body is mobilized to do one thing and one thing only: survive.

BE FEARLESS: *In the face of fear, the fearless thrive while the fearful retreat.*

Many people think of the fear response as a negative response, and they want to eliminate it. The BE FEARLESS program will show you how to rethink that negativity. Your fear response can actually become a strength, one that you can harness and use to your advantage. Isn't it great, for instance, to know that you are capable of much more physical strength than you realize? If you were stuck under a heavy object, that extra strength generated by your fear response would surely come in handy. And if a tidal wave were coming your way, isn't it good to know that you would be able to run faster than you have ever run in your entire life? It's the same if someone were chasing you. You'd have speed that you didn't even know you had. I'm not a runner, but if I were being chased by a guy with a chain saw, you can bet that I'd be flying faster than I ever could imagine I'd be able to.

The fear response can also come in handy during non-life-threatening situations. You can turn fear into a strength when delivering a speech or keeping the conversation going during a first date. The BE FEARLESS program will show you how.

How the Contagion Effect Creates Fear

It's also our primitive, instinctual nature to spread fear. In the days of early humans, if danger lurked, one person would tell the next and the next and then the whole clan was notified. This still happens in the animal world. When one deer, for instance, senses danger, it lifts and waves its tail. Other deer do the same, alerting the entire group that danger lurks.

It's this instinctual response coupled with modern technology that can cause fear to go viral. With the push of a button, in a split second, the entire world is informed of information. Think of what happened with the swine flu epidemic or as the Y2K paranoia unfolded. Think of how you learned about terrorism attacks and more. Have you ever forwarded a scary e-mail to scores of friends? Have you ever passed along a scary rumor? Then you helped to spread the fear.

Not all of this viral fear is even based on reality. We get e-mails, texts, and other messages forwarded to us that warn us about hypodermic needles found on movie theater seats, that the growth hormones injected into chicken wings causes ovarian cancer in women, and that thieves are robbing women in shopping mall bathrooms and leaving them naked.

Are you feeling a little fearful just reading this litany of doom and gloom? I'm feeling fearful just typing it! The BE FEARLESS program helps you to overcome the Contagion Effect in several ways. It shows you how to inoculate yourself from the worst sources of fear. Perhaps most powerfully, the program teaches you how to deal with Fearmongers, those people in your life who spread fear, reinforce your negativity, and attempt to keep you stuck. You'll learn how to protect yourself from such people so you can reduce your fear and change your life for the better.

How You'll Override Your Fear Instinct

Just because fear is instinctual and genetic, it doesn't mean you can't face it, weaken it, or even use it to your advantage. You can do something about your fear. There's a solution.

BE FEARLESS will teach you how to create more certainty in an uncertain world. This program helps you map out your future so you can create as much certainty as possible.

In addition to creating certainty, this program will teach you how to systematically face your fear, befriend it, and use it to help you grow stronger. Each time you face your fear, you will be overwriting those negative reference experiences and old conditioning. In essence, you will be forming new memories that will fuel you with the confidence you need to continually face your fear again and again and again.

Fearlessness is not a lack of fear. Rather, it's acting in the face of it. The program in this book teaches you how to do just that.

Change Your Life Now!

We all suffer from a negativity bias that causes us to remember negative events over positive ones and predict negative outcomes over positive ones. Start challenging your negativity bias now. Whenever you notice yourself making negative predictions—*he's just not that into me, my mother is going to flip out, my boss is going to hate this report, my friends are already irritated with me*—check your thinking. **Ask yourself:**

- Is there another, just-as-plausible explanation?
- Is it just as possible that everything will turn out okay?
- Why am I so confident that things will not turn out okay?
- Am I basing a future prediction on one past event?

Also, keep a written tally of how often your negative predictions come true. I think you will be pleasantly surprised to see that most of them just don't and that the positive far outweighs the negative.

Chapter Three

What Keeps Fearful People Stuck

Before coming to see me, many of my clients were stuck. They wanted to change their lives, but they couldn't seem to move forward. Initially they thought that it was their fate to lead an unfulfilling life. As it turned out, however, their problems had nothing to do with fate and everything to do with fear-inducing coping styles that were holding them hostage.

Over the years, I've been able to identify thirteen fearful coping styles that keep people stuck and stop them from pursuing their dreams. You'll read about them in the following pages. Interestingly, people generally turn to these tactics in an attempt to reduce or avoid fear, but these tactics tend to backfire and intensify fear instead. The BE FEARLESS program will help you to break out of these fear-inducing coping styles so you can finally move forward and create the life you were meant to live.

The BE FEARLESS Solution

The table that follows illustrates these thirteen dysfunctional coping styles and offers highly effective strategies for each.

Fearful Coping Style	*BE FEARLESS Prescription*
Venting	Define where you want to go rather than complain about where you currently are. (Step 1)
Ineffective therapy	Embark on a program that breaks you out of perpetual venting and encourages you to face your fear and change your life. (Steps 1–5)
Medication	Learn how to control and override your fear response. (Step 4)
Wishful thinking	Create an action plan that gets you from Point A (now) to Point B (the life you want). (Step 5)
Avoiding your fear	Face your fear in small, nonthreatening doses that allow you to continually achieve success, build courage, and move forward. (Step 5)
Fixating on problems	Continually search for solutions. (Step 3)
Negativity	Reframe negative thoughts into motivating, positive statements. (Step 3)
Controlling the uncontrollable	Control the controllable. (Steps 2 and 3)
Giving up at failure	Reframe failure and create small successes. (Steps 3 and 5)

Fearful Coping Style	BE FEARLESS Prescription
Being comfortable with fear	Overcome your codependent relationship with fear. (Step 2)
Overthinking	Embark on your action plan. (Step 5)
People pleasing	Distance yourself from Fearmongers. (Prep Task #3)
Societal Brainwashing	Fearproof your Dream List. (Step 1)

Fearful People Vent About Their Problems

Rachel had been seeing her therapist for years, but she wasn't getting better. She was still just as fearful and anxious as she'd been before her first appointment.

Her friend Linda, however, also had fear and anxiety issues, and she had gotten better after just a few months of seeing me. Rachel wondered how Linda had overcome her issues so quickly.

Are my issues more extreme? she wondered. *Maybe I'm more screwed up than Linda is.*

She suspected, however, that a different reason was to blame. Could it be that her therapy was ineffective?

Rachel decided to find out. She called to ask me a few questions. She told me that she'd been seeing her current therapist for six years.

"How's that going?" I asked.

"Well, it's good to vent," she replied.

"What have you gained by venting for six years?" I asked.

"Well I haven't gotten worse," she said. "It feels good to vent."

Oh, the "it's good to vent" line. I can't tell you how many times I've heard that line, especially from clients, like Rachel, as they describe their old therapy. The problem is that venting is merely a way to get temporary relief. It doesn't teach clients the strategies they need to get better. Case in point: before seeing me, these clients had been mired in therapy for years. For them, the patient-therapist relationship was one of codependence: the patient depended on the therapist for emotional support, and the therapist depended on the patient for money. The patients had a need to feel listened to and heard. The therapists had a need to pay their overhead and even for their summer vacations. To keep the patients coming back, the therapists would warn them of all of the horrific emotional consequences that might befall them if they stopped the therapy.

End result: the patients never got better.

I've heard this story way too many times from clients who talk about their former therapists. It's frustrating. Aren't therapists supposed to help people? Why instill fear by telling a patient that she can't stop the therapy? What a tragedy!

When I first counseled Rachel, I said, "There's a difference between feeling better and actually getting better. I want you to get better."

She wanted to get better too.

I explained that my approach was different, that I wasn't one of *those* types of therapists. I didn't just nod my head and listen as clients talked about their problems. Rather, I helped them do something about those problems. My approach was engaging. It was interactive. I gave homework, and I held my clients accountable with the goal of getting better.

I suggested Rachel come in for an appointment, and I asked her to bring a list of her goals for therapy.

At the first meeting Rachel told me that she was overworked in her high-stress job in sales, was unhappy in her current relationship, lacked confidence, and was fearful of marriage given her parents' divorce. None of it seemed like something that would require six years of therapy. We talked a little about her issue of the day: she didn't know how to get her boyfriend to attend her work functions, and she was growing increasingly frustrated and depressed about it.

"What have you tried?" I asked.

"I tell him he should be going with me because he's my significant other. Each time he tells me he's busy, that he has his own obligations and events to attend, and that he's never bothered me to attend his events with him," she said.

I knew right away what was wrong with her approach. It was demanding, negative, and uninspiring. Why *would* he want to go?

I asked, "Would you attend his event if he asked you the way you ask him?"

A look came over her face that sort of said, *Oh my.*

I gave her some paper and asked her to write down all the reasons she wanted her boyfriend to join her beyond just "because he's my significant other." She wrote things such as, "He's charming. He gets along well with a lot of people. It would give him an opportunity to meet my colleagues and understand my job better. It would be fun to get out and break up the workweek routine."

She had never told him any of this.

We then did some role-playing designed to help her learn how to approach him in a positive way. As the session wound down, I gave her homework:

1. Write out your strengths.
2. Write out how you think your boyfriend perceives you.

I told her I was confident I could help her and asked if she had any questions. She had a smile on her face and also looked a bit perplexed.

"Is everything okay?" I asked.

"I've gotten more out of this single session than I've gotten out of six years with my other therapist," she said.

"What made you want to try a new therapy approach?" I asked.

"A few weeks ago I asked my therapist if he had any advice. He answered, 'See you next week.' That's when I realized that things weren't going anywhere and that they never would."

Hers, unfortunately, is a common story. It's the norm, not the exception.

Test It Out

Survey ten of your friends. Ask them what they think therapy is all about. I'm guessing that nine out of ten people will tell you that therapists are sounding boards and that therapy is about venting and being listened to.

Fearful People Stay Stuck in Therapy

I've listened as client after client told me that I was their fifth or eighth or eleventh therapist. I've seen clients who have seen other therapists for twelve years and who have not gotten better! They tell me about therapists who just nod their heads and say little to nothing, who continually glance at the clock during the session, who doze off, and who worry more about getting paid than about solving a patient's issues.

My therapy is results oriented, has a purpose, and holds clients accountable to the goals. All too often, however, therapy keeps people trapped within their fear. It perpetuates problems and it reinforces negative behavior. Because the clients never get instructions on how to move forward, they are held hostage by the therapy. Therapists keep them talking endlessly about their problems and fears rather than coaxing them to do something about them.

It's sad. Every time I hear stories about therapists who don't get people better, I think, *Wow, why are people paying money for this?* If your hairstylist kept giving you a bad cut, would you keep going back? If a restaurant served you food that didn't taste good and left you hungry, would you make another reservation? You wouldn't continue to go to a fitness trainer if you were not getting into shape, would you?

No, I'm sure you wouldn't.

Yet people keep going back to therapists who don't help. They don't do this because they enjoy staying stuck. They do it because they don't know any better. They think that they are too messed up to get better. They don't realize that there is a better approach. They assume that all therapists are supposed to act as sounding boards. So week after week they go back, even though they are not becoming more self-sufficient and even though they don't learn skills that help them cope with their lives. Problems are perpetuated. This, in part, is my motivation for writing this book. I want people to get better and not waste time and money on therapy that doesn't work.

If you are seeing the wrong therapist, you can end up becoming more dependent rather than less. The therapist may be the only person in your life who listens and who pays attention to you. Your therapist may be the only person you can vent to. This makes you feel special, so you feel good when you leave. But do know that there's a difference between feeling good and getting better and that difference is what stands between you and success.

Your therapist listens, which validates you, but this validation comes at a high cost! Let's do the math. If you are paying out of pocket, then an average session costs about $100. Multiply that by 52 weeks and then by 5 years, and you've paid out $26,000. You could have flown yourself and a guest first-class to Paris, France, and have stayed at the Four Seasons, one of the most expensive hotels in the world, for a week.

Let's say you have insurance and are only doling out a $20 co-pay—the ineffective therapy still comes at a high price. That's $20 × 52 weeks × 5 years = $5,200. Just think of what else you could have spent that money on!

That's a lot of time and a lot of money for a service that isn't getting you better. You could get the same validation—for a lot less money—by telling your problems to your dog or even to a pet rock.

I'm not against therapy. After all, I practice it. But there are probably more bad therapists than good ones. Fearful people stay mired in bad therapy. Fearless people change therapists if the therapy isn't working.

If you are in therapy or are thinking of using therapy as an adjunct to this book, you don't want to keep going back to a therapist who simply listens and never tells you what to do, and you don't want to keep going back to a therapist who keeps asking you questions about your potty training days. Interview a number of therapists to get a sense of their beliefs and approach. Ask them questions like, "How can you help me?" and "What strategies will you use to help me overcome my fear?"

Use this advice when looking for a therapist:

- **Use the speed dating approach.** Meet many, interview them about their style and beliefs, and settle on one that seems like a good fit for you.
- **Look for someone who is results oriented.** Ask, "How do you plan to help me?" You might also ask, "How long does

your average client stay in therapy?" and "What tools do you plan to teach me to help me cope?"

- **Identify your goals.** Tell potential therapists what you expect to get out of therapy. Be specific, suggest the therapist find a way to monitor your progress, and set a date when you both can expect for you to see results.

Fearful People Look for a Magic Pill

The idea of speaking in public causes a great deal of anxiety for many people. Some people just avoid it, a strategy that only strengthens the fear. More and more, however, I'm hearing from people who tell me, "Oh, I don't have a problem with public speaking. I just pop a Xanax beforehand and I'm fine."

A Xanax?

Xanax (alprazolam), Ativan (lorazepam), and Klonopin (clonazepam) are medications that are used to treat anxiety and panic attacks. They work by calming the brain, but common side effects include drowsiness, light-headedness, fatigue, and difficulty concentrating. Is that really how you want to feel just before giving a speech? It's definitely not how I would want to feel! I personally would want to feel clearheaded, energetic, and focused.

We live in a society that is obsessed with quick fixes. When we gain weight, we want a magic pill, a shake, or liposuction to help us get skinny again. Rather than save money over the years, we play the lottery. Instead of getting more sleep, we reach for caffeine.

Thanks, in part, to advertising, the idea of quick fixes permeates our thinking. You can't turn on the TV late at night and not be confronted by an infomercial for a product designed to shrink the fat, remove years from your face, or help you get rich overnight.

Still, as my dad always says, "If it sounds too good to be true, it probably is." Using anti-anxiety medications to overcome fear is too good to be true. Pills might numb you, but they don't provide insight and tools to help you solve your problems.

More worrisome is that they could make your problems even worse. For instance, what if you had to speak in public and you didn't have the pill that you've come to rely on? Let's say you were in a meeting and your boss called on you. Or let's say you were at a convention and you were suddenly asked to fill in for a no-show. How would you cope? Would you fall apart? Or would you turn down the opportunity just because you didn't have a pill to help you get through it?

I have the same question for just about any fear you think medication might help ease. I know many people who pop a pill before a date, for instance. But what if you meet someone at a social event? What will you do without your anti-anxiety pill? Will you choke? Will you sweat through it? Or will you run and hide?

Similarly, I know a few people who take pills to overcome a fear of flying. You might initially think, *What's the problem?* After all, it's not as if most people fly every single day. Why not rely on a pill to get yourself through an experience you have to confront only once or twice a year? Here's why. What happens if your flight is delayed and doesn't take off until your pill has worn off? This very thing happened to a friend of mine. Her spouse carried her onto that plane while she cried, screamed, and kicked. Here's another situation: What happens if the plane has to make an emergency landing? Or what happens if another passenger is in crisis? Won't you want to be able to react quickly in these situations? Would you really be able to keep your wits about you if you are under the influence of a tranquilizer?

Anti-anxiety medications do not solve your problems, and they do not teach you how to face and overcome fear. They do not give you insights into what's wrong with your life. Worse, they are habit-forming and often pose side effects that reinforce your fear. For instance, are you really going to be a good conversationalist during a first date if you are numb because of an anti-anxiety medication?

My new clients who relied on Xanax and other anti-anxiety medications before coming to see me have complained that they can't get past the first date. They've told me that they are undesirable and undatable. In every case, however, I've found that they are not undesirable at all. Their coping strategy was. Once they found the courage to ditch the anti-anxiety medications, they stopped behaving like boring, lifeless duds and started behaving like their true selves. Date one soon turned into date two and then date three and onward.

Similarly, by popping a pill before giving a speech, you ensure that you are going to give a mediocre speech. The audience will respond accordingly, strengthening your fear. On the other hand, if you learned how to give a speech without relying on medication, you'd be able to do it with energy and a clear head. The probability of you really engaging the audience is much higher. As a result, the audience will respond by paying attention, asking questions, laughing, clapping, and thanking you. All of this is going to make you think, *I don't know why I was so scared to do that. This isn't that bad.* That's all much-needed positive reinforcement.

Unfortunately, physicians are way too quick to prescribe these pills, and people are way too quick to ask for them. Every week someone new comes to me and says, "I went to my primary care doctor. I told him that I was feeling anxious. Within five minutes he gave me a prescription."

That's our society. I often ask physicians, "If you didn't have a prescription pad, how would you treat the problem?" They look dumbfounded. When all you have is a hammer, everything you see looks like a nail. When all you have is a prescription pad, every patient you see needs a pill.

> ### *Think About It*
>
> What do you think would happen if you went to your primary care
> doctor and complained of feeling sad, having trouble getting out
> of bed, being under a lot of stress, and not feeling like yourself?
> How long do you think it would take before your doctor suggests
> medication? I bet you would walk out with a prescription.

Whenever I have a client who is on several medications, one
of my main goals is to help that person wean him- or herself off
the pills. Most of the time, I am successful so long as the person
is motivated and willing to work hard.

Obviously there are some cases where people really need these
medications. In the vast majority of cases, however, people don't.
Most of the time, a doctor has prescribed these serious medications
to treat the equivalent of a psychological sniffle. That's like giving
morphine for a paper cut. It's unnecessary and possibly even harmful.

If you are currently taking medications, don't stop without
talking to your doctor. Just know that they are not necessarily
the answer. To truly overcome your fear, you must be open to
learning new ways to cope.

> ### *Think About It*
>
> If you take anti-anxiety medications to cope with a fearful situ-
> ation, think about how you would face that fear if anti-anxiety
> medications were not an option. What would you do? If you had
> a friend who took medications in order to cope with a specific
> fear, what advice would you give your friend for dealing with that
> fear without the help of medication?

Fearful People Wish Things Were Better

In the mega bestseller *The Secret*, Rhonda Byrne writes about what she calls the Law of Attraction. According to this law, you can attract good or bad outcomes to yourself. You can "manifest" anything you desire as long as you know specifically what you want and think about it diligently enough. According to *The Secret*, you just have to visualize what you want, ask for it, believe you already have it, and behave as if it is already there in your life.

If you want to be rich, for instance, you would envision what it might be like to be rich. You would ask the universe to make you rich. You would frame a fake million-dollar bill, hang it on the wall, and stare at it every day. And you would do things that rich people do. For instance, you would buy designer handbags. Soon money would pour into your bank account.

It's tempting to want to believe that getting what you want could be so easy and so stress free. Don't believe this even for a second. Change takes desire, but it also takes a strategy, hard work, and perseverance.

BE FEARLESS: *Fearless people don't wish for change. They create it.*

When I was a kid I used to bury my head in my pillow, close my eyes, and imagine that I was Superman or Luke Skywalker. When I squeezed my eyes shut, I was always a hero. In these fantasies, I flew to rescue the Lois Lanes in my life at the time. This would go on, and on, and on, and it worked—as long as I kept my head buried in that pillow and my eyes squeezed shut.

As soon as I opened my eyes and faced real life, I was as wimpy as I'd always been. Wishing to be a hero didn't make me one.

This magical thinking made me feel good and gave me a wild, if not even a delusional, sense of self. But in the end, no matter how much time I spent with my face buried in that pillow, I never did fly or save the damsel in distress.

Similarly, for years I've dreamed of having big bulging biceps. I've envisioned these biceps *for years*. To this day, they remain rail thin. Did I not wish for them hard enough? I don't think so. My guess is that if I would set aside time, consult a trainer, and get pumping, I would get a little definition to my biceps. You can't wish your biceps bigger. You make your biceps bigger. It's the same with everything else you want in life. *The Secret* encourages you to have a vision, and that's important. You need a vision. But you also need a strategy and an action plan—two important ingredients to success that *The Secret* doesn't provide.

Test It Out

Now I'm not telling you that you have to stop all forms of wishful thinking, but I am telling you that you might want to consider additional options. If you are a fan of the Law of Attraction, I'd like you to think long and hard about these questions:

- How is wishful thinking working for you?
- Without any effort on your part, has wishful thinking ever magically made a dream of yours come true?

I'm guessing it hasn't. If it had, you'd still be relying on those techniques and you wouldn't be holding this book in your hands.

To help you see the difference, let's talk about my dreams for this book. Now, like all authors, I'd really like the masses to love this book. I dream of reaching and helping millions and seeing the book land on the *New York Times* best-seller list. According to *The Secret*, all I need to do is ask for it and believe in it, and I shall receive. You know, I fell for that for about a microsecond. Then I realized there's a huge difference between wishing, fantasizing, and magically thinking, and smart hard work with a strategy. Had I done only the former, you wouldn't be reading this book right now.

What I did do was this: I had a plan with specific steps to take toward that final goal. This of course started with healthy visualization. I visualized the actual steps to take to reach my goal rather than just visualizing the end result. I saw myself, for instance, carve out a catchy angle, collaborate with an expert writer, surround myself with smart people who could guide me, sell the proposal, write the rest of the book, and then come up with a marketing plan. In the BE FEARLESS program, you will do a similar visualization and form an action plan so you can face your fear and reach your goals.

Test It Out

If you were in college, which method do you think would be more likely to help you achieve a perfect 4.0 grade point average?

- Staring at a piece of paper that had the number 4.0 written on it in big block letters.
- Diligently going to class, studying the material, and meeting the professor during office hours as needed.

It's the second, right? This is true of every life goal or dream you can possibly come up with. Action equals success.

Wishful thinking is usually an outgrowth of a fear. People don't resort to wishful thinking because it works. They resort to wishful thinking because it allows them to avoid confronting their fear.

Wishful thinking allows you to avoid discomfort, stress, change, anxiety, and pressure. It's a lot easier and less stressful to stare at a fake check for a million dollars than it is to ask your boss for a raise or to work hard. But which method is more likely to result in more money flowing into your bank account? The more stressful one.

People resort to prayer, wishful thinking, and magical thinking when they are afraid of bad outcomes. For instance, they avoid the doctor out of fear and pray for good health instead. They refuse to open their credit card bills out of fear, and they wish for wealth instead. They do not approach people they would like to date, but they attempt to mentally manifest their perfect mate by wishing for him, cleaning out a closet for him, and imagining him. They are fearful they won't be a success, so they resort to wishing they would write that book instead of actually writing one.

Naturally, in the face of fear, it's easier to think about fantasy than to think about reality.

Think About It

Visualize all of the steps you think you might have to take in order to get to your goal. Close your eyes and see what you will do first, second, and third. For instance, if you want to become a more confident public speaker, visualize yourself learning how to present your material, practicing ahead of time, waiting to go onstage, and then delivering the actual speech. Don't just watch the end: the audience giving a standing ovation. Make sure to see the beginning and middle too.

Also, think about ways you can make what you want to come true. How can you make your dreams a reality? What are the fears that are causing you to wish for success and happiness rather than actually pursuing it?

Fearful People Avoid What Scares Them

This is probably the most common way people deal with fear, and it seems to make intuitive sense. After all, why would you move toward something that is painful or threatening? You wouldn't, for instance, jump off a bridge no matter how many times I told you, "Oh, just do it, everything will be fine!" You wouldn't light yourself on fire either. In these situations your fear would stop you *for a good reason.* It would prevent you from choosing certain death in a life-or-death situation.

The problem, however, is that most fears are not about life or death. For instance, I don't know anyone who has died from giving a speech, from forcing himself onto the dance floor, or from approaching a woman and asking her on a date.

Such situations don't kill us. The anxiety, especially if it progressed into a panic attack, might cause you to feel as if you were dying, but no one ever has died from a panic attack either. Eventually the panic goes away.

Because fear feels so scary, many people run in the other direction as they tell themselves things like *I can't speak in front of a crowd* and *I can't dance* and *I can't ask for a raise.*

In reality, however, you can. For the vast majority of situations, the fear isn't based in reality. It's all in your head, and it's not as scary as it might initially seem.

BE FEARLESS: *You can feel nervous and still be okay. It's scarier to hide from fear than it is to face it and deal with it.*

You might argue that you don't have to face these fears, that avoiding them isn't harming you. The problem with this thinking is twofold. For one, it's probably difficult to completely avoid your fear. Sure, if you have a fear of snakes, you might be able to get through most of your life without confronting them. But many other fears are a completely different story. For instance, I have a fear of dancing. I didn't confront it because I didn't think I had to. It's not as if I find myself on a dance floor every day. Then not long ago, I attended my cousin's wedding. She asked me to dance. I felt so anxious that I turned her down. The bride asked me to dance with her and I refused! What kind of a person am I? Days later I wished that I'd faced that fear.

Second, the longer you avoid facing your fear, the bigger it grows. By avoiding it, you are telling yourself, *This is scary.* The avoidance and self-talk reinforces the fear itself, allowing it to grow stronger and become even more debilitating.

Think About It

Think about everything you are missing out on because of what you are avoiding. How much richer could your life become if you didn't feel the need to hide from your fear? What would you be able to do? Suppose you were not fearful—how would your life be?

Fearful People See Problems

Many years ago, when I was a graduate student, I lived in the Bronx. I took the subway back and forth to Manhattan regularly and usually late at night. The train took me through some of the highest-crime areas of New York City. My landlord had told me not to take the train at night because of various crime problems. As a result, I felt a great deal of fear. I worried, perhaps rightly so, that someone might try to mug me.

I couldn't avoid the trip. I needed to get to and from Manhattan, and I didn't have the means to move to a different neighborhood or to take a taxi. So I thought about ways to make myself seem untouchable. I wanted to become the kind of passenger no one wanted to mess with. I'm tall and lanky, so physical intimidation was out. I knew I could never in a million years make someone think, *That guy might kick my ass.*

What are your strengths? I wondered. I thought about how I was in school learning to be a psychotherapist, and I was studying mental illness. I knew a lot about this topic, but most people knew little. I knew that people were afraid of what they didn't know, and that mental illness was often misunderstood. Although the mentally ill are often quite harmless, many people find them quite scary because of what they don't know and don't understand. As I devised my strategy, I counted on this uncertainty.

What do most people do when they encounter someone who seems mentally ill? I wondered. *What do they do when they see someone who is talking to him- or herself?*

They keep their distance, right? No one messes with a guy like that!

So as I stood on the subway platform, I paced, shook my head, talked to myself, and did my best impersonation of someone who was hearing voices and seeing objects and people that were not really there.

It worked. No one ever approached me! As a matter of fact, people *avoided* me. They were actually fearful of me. Imagine that.

Now, that might not be the strategy you would choose for such a situation. Still, it worked for me, and it's an example of solution-oriented thinking. I could have told myself, *I'm a wimpy guy. I'm an easy target. I have to move.* I could have focused on that problem and allowed it to incapacitate me.

Instead, I focused on possible solutions. You will learn to do the same in this book.

Think About It

Are you seeing your fear as an insurmountable problem? Could you use your fear to come up with a solution instead? Think differently. Be creative. Change your thinking so you can see solutions where you once only saw problems.

Fearful People Focus on the Negative

As I've mentioned, fear is about the unknown. It's about uncertainty. Our mind doesn't have all the answers, so it tries to fill in the blanks via a plausible story about what might happen. For people who are held hostage by fear, this story is usually negative. If a woman doesn't hear from a guy she is dating for a couple of days, for instance, she will think, *He must be married* or *He doesn't like me.* Her uncertain mind takes her straight to the worst-case scenario.

As you've learned, this is due to our negativity bias. Negative information has a greater impact on the brain than positive information, and it's processed much more quickly also.

Test It Out

Put several images of faces on paper or a computer screen. Make smiley faces, angry faces, sad faces, and so on. Show these images all at once to various people. You'll find that they'll notice the angry (negative) faces before the happy or positive faces.

So, what does all this mean when it comes to being fearless? Can you overcome your negativity bias? Yes, and that's exactly what fearless people have taught themselves to do. When they notice that they are predicting a negative outcome, they ask themselves, *Is this an accurate prediction? Is there another possible explanation? How do I know this is really happening?*

> **BE FEARLESS:** *Fearless people confront their negative thinking. When their mind pulls up a worst-case scenario, they ask themselves,* Where's the evidence?

It's okay to think negatively. It's normal, natural, and programmed into us. What I'd like you to do is just be aware of it. When you notice that your mind has gone negative, try not to dwell on it or fixate on it. Just acknowledge it and then see if you can push your mind to the positive. For example, the inner dialog of a fearful person who is stuck in traffic might go like this, *I can't believe I'm stuck in traffic. This is terrible. I'm going to be late and everyone is going to be mad at me. Gosh, I hope I don't get fired. What if I get fired? What will I do?*

A fearless person, however, would have a much different inner dialog. It would go like this, *Yes it's a bummer that I'm stuck in traffic and that I am going to be late to work. I hate being late, but I can contact the office and let them know.*

To understand how to change your thoughts from negative to positive, let's look at an example from a client I once counseled. Kristen was afraid to speak up at business meetings. Whenever she was called upon to speak, her voice would shake and her face would become flushed. This is how my initial conversation with Kristen went.

Me: "What goes through your mind when they call on you?"
Kristen: "I don't have anything smart to say. They will judge me."
Me: "Why do you think they ask you to speak at the meetings?"
Kristen: "I don't know . . . maybe they want to hear what I have to say."

Me: "Why else might they ask you?"

Kristen: "Maybe they want to hear my opinion. Maybe they want to know my ideas."

Me: "This isn't seventh grade, where the teacher is trying to grade you. This is work. I think you are right. I think they really do just want to hear what you have to say. They want to know what your ideas are and they value what you have to say. They are not grading you."

Kristen: "You're probably right."

I suggested that meetings really weren't about her at all. Rather, they were about information. "They are not judging you when you are talking," I said. "They are just listening."

I told her that whenever she caught herself thinking, *They will judge me,* she should tell herself the following over and over again, *They asked me to talk because they think I have something to contribute. They love what I have to say. They value my opinion.*

This is called reframing. The BE FEARLESS program encourages you to use reframing a lot and with any number of negative thoughts that you might have. You don't want to ignore the negative. It's there for a reason, and by attempting to ignore it you may strengthen your fear instead. So acknowledge the negative. This satisfies the part of your brain that needs to assess risk should you truly be in a life-or-death situation and flight should really be necessary.

Think About It

Look at the following thoughts. Which ones do you think would make you feel fearful? Which ones would help you feel more fearless? I've filled in some reframes for you. See if you can come up with your own reframes for the last five negative thoughts.

Negative Thoughts	Positive Thoughts
They are going to judge me.	They want to hear what I have to say.
Oh, no. I'm getting anxious. This isn't good.	Good, I feel excited. I'll be able to use this. This is motivating.
I am out of my comfort zone. What if I choke?	This is such a great opportunity. I can't wait to give this my all.
I'm a wimp.	I'm a sensitive, soft-spoken person.
Dating sucks.	Dating is an adventure.
She'll never like a guy like me.	
People will think I'm stupid and boring.	
This bridge is going to collapse.	
I'll never be a success.	
I'll make a fool out of myself.	

Fearful People Drive from the Passenger Seat

Have you ever been a passenger in a car with an inexperienced driver? Then you know just how out of control it feels when a driver doesn't brake quickly enough as a red light or an obstacle approaches. Maybe you've even slammed on the imaginary brake on the passenger side of the car a few times to no avail.

Fearful people live their lives as if they are passengers in an out-of-control car. Rather than doing something to control the situation—by getting into the driver's seat—they operate the car as passengers. They attempt to control what is out of their control, rather than what actually is within it. For instance, they worry about the economy and whether the latest government solution will work—despite the fact that they have little, if any, control over such a situation.

As a result, they feel victimized.

Fearless people do the opposite. When in the middle of what might initially seem like an uncontrollable situation, they shift the locus of control from what they can't change to what they can.

For instance, if your company is downsizing and you are afraid of losing your job, you might not be able to control how many positions get cut and whether yours is one of them. But you can take some actions to make you and your position less expendable. You can, for instance, control your relationship with your supervisor, your work performance, and whether you pursue continuing education outside of work to improve your skills and marketability.

If you have already lost your job, you might not be able to control how quickly you'll be able to find a new one. But you can control your daily schedule and maintain structure. For instance, you can still get up at the same time every day, shower, and get dressed and stick to a routine. You can make sure you read the job postings and apply for as many jobs as possible. You can network with colleagues in your area of interest. You can learn new skills that will make you more employable. You can even use this rare opportunity to get all of those things done around the house that you never had time to do.

Think About It

What area of your life feels out of your control? What are some ways you could exert more control over that area of your life? What can you control? What can't you? Use the chart below for ideas.

What You Can't Control	What You Can Control
Whether she will agree to have dinner with you.	What you wear, what you say, and how you say it when you make the request.
Whether you'll get a promotion.	How well you perform your job so that your supervisors see you as promotion worthy.
Whether you will die of a heart attack.	The foods you consume, how much and how often you exercise, and how much stress is in your life.
Whether the traffic you are stuck in will start moving in time for you to get to your appointment.	Whether you listen to traffic reports on the radio, whether you call in to the office to say you are stuck in traffic, what you do to entertain yourself while you are stuck.

Fearful People Stop at Failure

Earlier I told you about David and how he feared talking to women he found attractive. Just before he approached a woman, he thought about the last time he had gotten rejected. This made him think, *She's just going to reject me.*

His problem was that he was fixated on that one past rejection. Remember the negativity bias that I mentioned earlier? Well, this is a perfect example. He'd probably had plenty of positive experiences with women before that one rejection, but his negativity bias caused him to focus on this one rejection. The rejection became a negative reference experience for him, causing him to fear that the same negative outcome would happen again.

His is a common story. I've heard it from people who are afraid to pursue certain careers after getting fired. Many adults are afraid to drive on highways after having an accident. Many people became afraid to fly after the September 11, 2001, terrorist attacks. Some people are afraid to dance because of one bad experience they had way back in seventh grade when schoolmates made fun of their dorky dance moves.

The one bad reference experience gets transferred onto all new experiences, causing a pervading fear that can last for years if not faced with effective strategies.

If you continue to focus on a past negative experience, you won't be able to move forward. The only way to move forward is to replace the negative reference experience with positive, sequential successes. That's exactly what the BE FEARLESS program does. By helping you to learn from the past, the program enables you to create many successes now and in the future so you will no longer be held hostage by your fear of failure.

Test It Out

The fear that results from a negativity bias tends to have a self-fulfilling prophecy effect because it affects your expressions, tone of voice, and body language. You can see this for yourself. Spend one hour smiling at people, chatting, and generally seeming friendly, happy, and approachable. Spend another hour frowning, looking sad, and generally avoiding people. Notice how others around you react.

For David this meant he had to stop personalizing rejection. To do so, I asked him to believe: *I am stronger than just one rejection. One rejection doesn't mean that I am bad, unlovable, or ugly, or that I will never find love. All it means is that one person was not a match for me.*

I also had him change his beliefs. Not every woman in the world was going to dig him, and that was okay. I had him replace his negative self-talk with positive statements like *I'm a good-looking, career-driven professional.*

Finally, I encouraged him to create opportunities for small successes. He started by approaching a woman he did not find attractive—someone he would never usually date. I asked him to walk up to her and have a conversation. Nothing more. Once he could do that, he had one success. So we built in more. Eventually he was able to approach a woman he was interested in and ask her on a date! Women responded favorably. He had the positive reinforcement that he needed to move forward.

Think About It

Is there a negative reference experience that is keeping you fearful? What are some small positive steps you could take to overcome that negative experience? How can you create positive successes that will help prove that you have less to fear than you might initially think?

Fearful People Are Soothed by the Familiar

If you've ever had a friend who has stayed in a horrifically dysfunctional relationship, then you've thought, *Why doesn't she leave him?* Maybe you've had a friend who has done the same with a work situation. This friend constantly complains about her boss, her coworkers, and even the daily tasks. There's nothing redeeming about the job, yet she stays.

Why don't they get out?

Fear.

Humans, by nature, fear change. Once you become comfortable with any situation, it will begin to feel less threatening to you to maintain the status quo than it will to push the limits—even though pushing the limits is exactly what you need to do.

Most of us fear change to some degree and take steps to avoid it. The more you stay put, however, the more your fear of change will build and the harder it will become for you to move forward. Conversely, the more you nudge yourself forward, the easier it will become for you to embrace change in the future.

Yes, in the short term, change is stressful. It won't be easy to leave a job with a regular paycheck, a relationship you've been in for years, or the neighborhood you know but do not love. The unfamiliar will feel scary and stressful. This will be difficult. But the payoff is huge. Finding the courage to face the short-term stress of change removes you from having to endure the long-term misery of staying stuck.

BE FEARLESS: *Have you become comfortable being uncomfortable? If so, it's time to act.*

In addition to fear, there is probably at least one other factor that is holding you back. Despite how bad a situation you are in, you are probably benefiting from it in some way. For instance, people stay in unfulfilling jobs because they know the routine, are comfortable with the salary, and know how to work the system to some degree. If they leave, they must learn the ropes all over again and, for many people, that thought is daunting.

Further, people stay in relationships because it allows them to avoid dating. They don't have to worry about meeting and dealing with all of the other jerks they don't know, and they don't have to open themselves up to rejection. They can just deal with the one jerk already in their lives.

Think About It

What type of change might you be avoiding in your life? Why are you avoiding it? How are you benefiting from staying stuck? What are you gaining by giving in to your fear? What are you missing out on by not taking a risk?

Fearful People Think Too Much

I know a *New York Times* best-selling author who is really good at what she does. She has a proven record of success, including several media appearances. She's even been on the *Today* show. Still, there was this one show she really wanted to get on. It was the *Daily Show with Jon Stewart*. In her mind this was the ultimate show to be on, and she had made it out to be a lot more than it was.

I asked her what it meant to her to be on the show. She responded with these statements: *It would be the greatest accomplishment of my life. I have to get on. What's the point of trying? They'll never say yes.*

In her mind, she had turned this gig into something gigantic, imposing enormous pressure on herself. The way she dealt with this flood of emotions was to procrastinate and avoid what she thought would be a negative outcome. Instead of doing something that would actually result in possibly getting on the show, she did nothing.

"I think you are making this out to be bigger than it really is," I suggested. "Why don't you just pitch the show? What's the worst thing that could happen?"

"They could turn me down," she said.

I gently prodded. For months I asked her if she'd pitched the *Daily Show*. I even tracked down the phone number for one of the show's producers and sent it to her. But her story remained the same. My friend gave me one excuse after another for not pitching the show. These ranged from "the time isn't right" to "I have a publicist who is supposed to do this for me."

Finally, after months of excuses and procrastination, my friend sent in her pitch. She e-mailed me afterward, "That was a lot easier than I ever expected." She didn't get on the show (yet), but she taught herself an important lesson: procrastination doesn't make fear go away.

Hers is a common coping strategy for the fearful. Many people never move into action. They stare at the phone, but they don't dial it. They write the e-mail, but they don't send it. They want something. They put all of the pieces in place. Then they just can't seem to take the next step and jump. They think of all of the reasons why they shouldn't do it instead of all of the reasons they should. They think of all of the reasons someone will reject them and say no rather than all of the reasons someone might say yes. They keep saying, "Not yet," instead of saying "Let's do this now."

This is a form of procrastination, and it stems from a natural instinct to self-preserve. But there is also such a thing as too much thinking and too much analyzing. If you are hesitating and waiting for the right moment to strike, you are probably overthinking. If you keep thinking and never doing, you'll never reach your goal. For instance, had I procrastinated, I wouldn't have started writing an advice column, appeared on television, or ever written this book.

BE FEARLESS: *The longer you hesitate, the harder it will be to act. Don't think. Just do.*

The problem with procrastination is that it actually reinforces the anxiety. Each time you put off doing something, you are able to avoid the temporary anxiety of doing it. That makes you feel better, which reinforces the idea that thinking more and doing less is a good idea. It's not. The longer you think, the less likely it is that you will ever turn all of those thoughts into action.

In the face of challenges, real or imagined, the fearless persevere. They know that facing their anxiety is scary and it hurts. But they also know that this pain is temporary. Once they get past it, they will feel more powerful. They live by a phrase I coined and often say to my clients: "Don't think. Just do."

Think About It

Do you move easily into action? Or do you tend to psych yourself out by telling yourself all of the reasons you shouldn't move forward? Think of all of the reasons you should do something, why you want to do something, and why you will do something. Stop thinking of all of the reasons you shouldn't do it. Think about all of the reasons why you should. Then do it.

Fearful People Can Be Too Nice

Carol came to see me for stress and mild depression. She was thirty-nine, married, had two kids, and held a professional job dealing with contracts for a major company. She came to see me at the urging of her sister, who noticed she was stressed out. Carol was well-spoken, careful about how she interacted with me, very proper, kind, and respectful.

I asked her to look into insurance coverage for her therapy and she did it right away. She ended up spending a lot of time on the telephone with her insurance provider, and did it despite her busy schedule. She found out everything that I'd asked her to find. Rarely do clients get it right, but she did. For that I was pleased. As I got to know her, however, a theme began to emerge.

Carol was willing to drop everything and anything to help others. She was a *People Pleaser*. People Pleasers go above and beyond the call of duty, and they do this consistently. If a loved one passes away while a work deadline is looming, they will skip the funeral in order to meet the deadline. Or they will attempt to do both—at the expense of their own rest, peace of mind, and well-being. They put everyone and everything ahead of themselves and their own needs.

I realized that Carol was the type of person I would like to hire to manage my office. People Pleasers like Carol are star employees. They are willing to do anything for the company, anything to make someone happy, and anything to help anyone in need.

But people like this should not be exploited. And while kindness is a fine quality, it should not come at the expense of one's needs and personal happiness. Carol was stretched so thin that she had little if any time for herself.

For a week, I asked Carol to keep track of and write down two things:

1. Her needs
2. How she spent her time

The result was remarkable. She had plenty of needs, but she hardly ever met them. She loved reading, but almost never did it.

She enjoyed time with her friends, but rarely saw them. She was signed up for a yoga class, but she hadn't attended it in months, and she frequently skimped on sleep in order to get more done. She had no private time or alone time.

At the same time, she was an overachiever at work, and she was a supermom too. She took care of her kids, managed the household, and cooked and cleaned—and she did it all without any outside help. The dynamic at home was such that her husband came to expect her to take care of the kids, prepare meals, clean, deal with the kids' homework and school issues, and so on, even though Carol worked a full-time job, just as he did.

She had become comfortable with such an arrangement. It made her feel good. She felt needed.

On the outside, she seemed competent and successful. On the inside, however, she was a mess. She acted as others had come to see her rather than as how she truly was. She had created an image of herself as a superachiever, and she was working hard to continue portraying it at the expense of her own peace of mind. She was afraid to be vulnerable or show any weakness. She was afraid to ask for help, and she was afraid to say no.

Are You a People Pleaser?

To see if you are a People Pleaser, jot the following down on a piece of paper or in a notebook.

Describe yourself: _____

Describe how others view you: _____

Describe how you would like other people to see you: _____

continued

If there is a vast difference between how you see yourself and how you think others see you, it will cause a great deal of anxiety. Chances are much of your People Pleasing stems from your desire to get people to see you differently than the way you really are. The more aligned your views of yourself are with how others see you, the happier you'll be.

For Carol, I knew it was time for the "If I Say No, Then What?" exercise. It went like this:

Me: "Suppose someone asks you for help and you say no. What will happen?"

Carol: "People won't like me. The house will fall apart. No one else will do the work."

Me: "Suppose you say no, can you create a new ending?"

Carol: "What do you mean?"

Me: "For instance, if someone asks you to volunteer at the same time as your yoga class, you might create a new ending by saying, 'No, I can't volunteer at that time, but I could do it another day.'"

Carol: "So, if my husband tells me that his family is visiting next week and wants me to clean the house, I can say, 'I can't do that today, but maybe we can plan an afternoon this weekend and work on it together.'"

Me: "Exactly!"

I then asked what would happen if she asked her husband for help. It became apparent she feared his response. She believed that her husband wouldn't like her if she asked for help.

I encouraged her to think about other reasons why her husband liked her. I then had her think about how else she could get the same outcome without sacrificing so much of her own time.

Slowly Carol was able to make some changes. Initially they were small ones. For instance, she asked her husband one night to wash the dishes while she got the kids ready for bed. Eventually Carol was able to ask her husband to watch the kids so she could take that yoga class she always skipped. After a while Carol was no longer basing her self-worth on others and how much she did for them. She learned what was acceptable and what wasn't. She was no longer a People Pleaser, and she put her needs first and foremost.

As Carol's story illustrates, there can be such a thing as being too nice to people, especially if it comes at the cost of your own needs and well-being. The BE FEARLESS program will help you to overcome your fear of disappointing others. The following advice will also help:

- **Don't focus on what you think you "should" do.** Instead focus on what you *want* to do.
- **Be willing to do what's best for you, even if that means others around you don't fully approve.** Your happiness matters just as much as the happiness of others.
- **Keep a tally of two things: your needs and how you spend your time.** Are you spending any time on your own needs? If not, reallocate your time resources so you are.
- **Continually ask yourself: "If I say no, then what?"** What will happen if you turn down requests for your help? What will happen if you take time for yourself? What will happen if you ask someone to help you so you can take time for yourself?

Think About It

Do you give because you are trying to gain a friend or because you genuinely want to share? If the latter, then giving should feel good and not interfere with what you need to do to be healthy and happy. If the former, you will probably find that you are filled with apprehension, anxiety, and eventually resentment when you give.

Think about how you could achieve the same outcome without giving too much. Think about a person you respect, someone who seems to take care of him- or herself. How does he or she do it?

Fearful People Have Been Brainwashed

Years ago, I thought I needed to work for others in order to fit in and be happy. I thought I needed a regular paycheck in order to feel secure. After all that's what society teaches us: go to school, get a degree, get a job, and stay there for thirty years.

Over time and after multiple jobs that didn't work out, I realized I didn't. I'd just been brainwashed by the idea that society dictates what I need in my life. I thought I was supposed to go to school, meet a girl, get married, have a kid, buy a house, and live happily ever after, because that's what other people did. I realized how unfulfilling that could all be for me if it came at the expense of me putting off my dreams or before I was ready.

I see this regularly in my clients, and I call it *Societal Brainwashing*. When they tell me that they hate their jobs, I suggest they think about a new profession. That's when they tell me that they can't walk away from the paychecks, lifestyle, prestige, and the titles. They essentially have grown comfortable with being uncomfortable.

Societal Brainwashing goes beyond just career issues. I see it in people who are in relationships too. For instance, I have counseled clients who would have been happier if they had remained single. They married before they were ready or they married someone who fell far short of their ideal mate.

> **BE FEARLESS:** *It's really okay to stand apart from others. You do not have to fit into society's expectations of you. Create your own healthy expectations.*

Societal Brainwashing causes us to believe that we need to do things a certain way because everyone else in society does it. Here are some statements that sound like Societal Brainwashing to me:

I have to get married by the time I'm thirty.
I need to become a parent by the time I'm thirty-five.
I have to make six figures by age forty.
I have to own a house.
I have to pursue a traditional college degree.
I have to work a 9-to-5 job.
I have to fit in.

Whenever I hear such statements from a client, I think, *Really? You do? Why is that?* For instance, for the ones who say they have to get married by a certain age, I tell them, "Don't let age determine marriage. Focus on finding the right partner. After all, it's better to be happily single than miserably partnered."

When you suffer from Societal Brainwashing, two parts of yourself are at war with one another. Your idealistic self battles with your practical self. The practical self gives you all of the reasons you should aim for the status quo—it tells you that you need security, for instance. Your idealistic self wants you to follow your dream or your bliss—which sometimes isn't practical, according to society.

It can be scary to ignore the practical in favor of the ideal. That's why BE FEARLESS shows you how to define your ideal future and then create a *practical* plan that will get you there. That's how you'll find the courage to take small and actionable steps toward your goal.

Change Your Life Now!

Are you stuck in any of these fearful patterns? Are you venting, overthinking, staying in therapy that isn't working, using medications to numb your nerves, avoiding what you fear or wishing it would just go away, people pleasing, or fixating on the negative, on past failures, or on what you can't control? If so, pull out a piece of paper. Create two columns. On one side, list all the reasons you don't want to stop using this coping strategy. On the other side, list all of the reasons this coping strategy is holding you back from following your dreams. Which reasons seem more worthwhile to you? Is it your need to be comfortable and go with the status quo that you already know isn't working for you? Or is it your desire to change and try a new approach?

Chapter Four

What Drives Fearless People Forward

What do you think of when you see a mountain climber? Or a skydiver? Or a gregarious networker? Or someone who seems comfortable speaking in front of a crowd?

You probably think that they were born fearless and that they do not feel the same anxiety and tension that you do.

What if I told you that you are wrong? What if I told you that they actually do feel fear? What if I told you that they were born with the same fear response that you were?

I'm guessing that you might not believe me at first. Yet it's true. The vast majority of people that most of us think of as fearless do feel anxious and nervous from time to time. Like you, their hearts pound. Like you, they experience other sensations that most of us associate with nervousness. For instance, their palms might sweat. Their mouths might go dry.

They feel fear, just as you feel fear.

In reality the difference between the fearful and the fearless is not the presence or absence of fear. The difference is this: the fearless interpret fear differently than the fearful do. When the fearless feel what most of us call "nerves," they don't think, *Oh, this is horrible. I'm getting nervous.* To the contrary, they accept nerves as a necessary part of life. Some fearless people even *enjoy* the very sensations that you currently fear. These so-called nerves make them feel alive. Nerves are what get them out of bed in the morning. Such fearless people find ways to use their fear response to their advantage. They turn those sweaty palms and racing heart rates into a strength.

Fearlessness is an attitude, a belief, and a lifestyle. When you decide to BE FEARLESS, you are not pledging to never again feel fear. No, what you are opting to do is embrace seven fearless behaviors and beliefs—the very behaviors and beliefs that are described in this chapter. The BE FEARLESS program is based on these seven behaviors and beliefs, and it will help you to develop and strengthen all of them. Once you do so, you will no longer feel set apart from the fearless. Rather you will have become one of them.

Fearless People Greet Fear at the Door

While giving a concert in Central Park in 1967, Barbra Streisand blanked on the words to three songs. After the concert, she kept thinking about those songs, playing that moment over and over in her mind. As she did so, the fear and anxiety built. She worried, *What if it happens again?*

Streisand is now one of the most successful entertainers in history, but back then she became so fearful of making such a mistake again that she limited her public performances for twenty-seven years!

I'm guessing that during those twenty-seven years Streisand learned what many fearless people have learned: Hiding doesn't make fear go away. Rather, it feeds the fear and makes it even worse.

Eventually Streisand did face her fear and finally agreed to sing at a large public event. Her performance went so well that she then went on a national tour and eventually performed in front of a large television audience.

During an interview with Oprah Winfrey, she said this about her stage fright, "I'll think, 'What am I doing on this stage? Holy mackerel!' But then I realize that fear has an energy behind it. The whole point is to go beyond the fear and do it anyway, because I know I'm singing for a good cause."

So you might be thinking, *Well sure, Streisand can face her fear. She's got enough money to pay a team of experts to help her. What about people who aren't so privileged? Isn't it harder and more impossible for us?*

I don't think that it is. I have a friend—a regular, everyday person—who doesn't have unlimited funds to spend on a team of people to help her with her mental health. Yet like Streisand, she too has been able to overcome what was once a debilitating fear of public speaking. She now sees that she was most fearful of public speaking during the many years she refused to do it. It was only after she began facing the fear that public speaking became less scary. In other words, facing it weakened the fear.

I've counseled countless people like you who all say the same. After a few sessions, they all—no matter their income, job status, or lifestyle—told me precisely what Streisand's quote conveys. It's easier to greet fear at the door than it is to hide in the closet and hope that the fear will go away. Fear doesn't go away unless you face it, and it only grows when you hide from it.

Fearless People Get Excited

When I met my coauthor, we were both waiting to go on television to talk about Tiger Woods cheating on his wife. I couldn't help but notice that Alisa was fidgeting and pacing. I boldly asked, "Do you get nervous before these TV appearances?"

"Yeah, a little," she said. "The worst part is that I sometimes get this nervous twitch in my cheek. I worry that other people can see it twitching."

She then did an imitation of what she thought she looked like with a nervous twitch. I could see how it might worry her. I then gave some unsolicited advice.

"Well, when you feel yourself getting nervous, instead of telling yourself that you are nervous, tell yourself that you are excited. They are the same sensations," I explained. "But when you interpret it as excitement, it's easier to deal with than if you interpret it as nerves."

Later, after we got to know one another better and began working on this book, she reminded me of that conversation.

"At first I thought there was no way something so easy and simple could possibly be even remotely effective," she said.

But she tried it while on air that day and it had seemed to help, she explained. At first she thought it was a fluke. Then she tried it again. And again. Soon she was feeling completely in control and confident.

It worked because fear and excitement are physiologically similar. The difference between the two is not in how your body feels but rather how your mind interprets it. When you tell yourself you are suffering from nerves, you reinforce the fear and end up having a negative experience. When you tell yourself that you are excited, you weaken the fear and turn what could have been a negative into a positive.

I first realized the power of this simple technique when I was trying to overcome my own fear of appearing on national television. Many years ago, my first television experience did not go as smoothly as I would have liked. I felt more nerves than I'd expected and, as a result, did not perform well.

I promised myself that I would not have a repeat performance like that ever again! I spent some time reflecting on it. I recognized what an awesome opportunity and privilege it was to be contacted by producers, reporters, and TV shows to offer *my* opinion. I wasn't a witness being cross-examined or a murder defendant in court. I had nothing to be afraid of. I was being given an opportunity to weigh in on newsworthy items. I was being asked what I thought about such items because people actually wanted to know. My opinion mattered! I thought to myself, *What a great opportunity I have. Of the several hundred thousand psychotherapists in the United States they could be tapping, these producers are calling me. Many people would love to be in my spot. But I'm the one here. This is so exciting!*

And it really was exciting. The more I thought about how great it was, the more excited I became.

And that was when I realized that the sensations of excitement are the same as the sensations of fear. The only difference was that I was thinking of fear as bad, which led to daunting,

overwhelming thoughts such as, *I can't believe this is happening!
I'm being judged! I'm such a mess!* On the other hand, I thought
of excitement as good, which led to more positive and motivating
thoughts like, *My body is ready. My mind is sharp. I'm alert and
on my toes.* If I embraced the fear and called it exciting, would I
feel more in control? I decided to find out.

The next few times I went on TV, I did something paradoxical.
Instead of trying to get myself as calm as possible, I psyched myself
up. I kept telling myself how great it was that I was at Rockefeller
Plaza, that I was in the very building where Dr. Ruth, my teenage heroine, got her start. As I felt the physiological reactions of
a dry mouth and a pounding heart, I didn't tell myself that they
were terrible and that I had to stop them. Instead I thought, *No
wonder I feel like this. I'm so excited to be here. This is how I
should be feeling.* And suddenly I found that I was able to be okay
with however my body felt, that no bodily sensation was going to
interfere with my ability to be my best.

Eventually I realized that fearless people do this somewhat
naturally. They feel what most of us call nerves, but they interpret
those sensations as excitement. For instance, I know someone who
loves to skydive, rock climb, and ride his mountain bike down the
sides of steep mountains. He seems fearless. When I asked him,
"Why do you do these things? Aren't you scared?" He replied, "It's
thrilling. I love the rush."

What he was calling a rush is what other people call nerves.

I've taught this very technique to hundreds of formerly fearful people, and it has worked for all of them. One of them was
Stephanie. In her early thirties, Stephanie was looking to meet a
guy and develop a meaningful relationship. She was tired of the
bar scene and frustrated with the lies fed to her by the men she
met through online dating sites. She told me that in their online
profiles these men regularly shed a few pounds, added a few inches

to their height, took a few years off, and even used pictures that were several years old. She could never figure out whether a guy really was who he said he was.

To give her a chance to meet several men, I suggested she attend a speed-dating event. Here, she'd be exposed to twenty men in just two hours. She would have an opportunity to speak to each one for three minutes and determine if she wanted to get to know them further. I often encourage my clients to try speed dating because, in my view, it gives you just enough time to see if someone is your type physically as well as decide whether you are interested in planning a potential date.

Stephanie loved the idea, but she also told me that she thought it was overwhelming and daunting. Just the idea of it led to anxiety and questions like *What if no one likes me? What if the guys are boring? What if the guys are ugly?* This fear-based anxiety was based on the unknown. She had lots of questions, lots of doubt, and a lack of confidence. But she tried it anyway.

At the next appointment, she told me that she'd experienced great fear and anxiety during the event. She'd had heart palpitations, an unsettled feeling, and sweaty palms. One of the guys had even commented on her slick palms. She'd embarrassingly replied, "It's hot in here."

I spent the session helping Stephanie to reframe the way she thought about speed dating. The goal was to help her to get excited for the opportunity rather than be fearful of things that might never even occur. I helped Stephanie to realize that she had a really good opportunity, one where she could potentially meet some great guys and not have to worry about whether they were lying about their age or looks. She was in control. I asked Stephanie, "How else can you meet twenty guys in two hours?"

When I met with her after her next speed dating attempt, there was a glimmer of excitement in her eyes. What she once feared she now saw as an exciting opportunity. This time she was able to make a joke about her sweaty palms, saying, "All these hot guys are making me sweat." She emerged feeling confident, realizing that she could take control of her anxiety, be relaxed, and be herself.

Think About It

Think of an activity that you find exciting and thrilling. Perhaps it's riding a roller coaster. Maybe it's white-water rafting. Maybe it's playing laser tag with your kids. Perhaps it's a special video game, one you find particularly challenging.

Whatever it is, think about how you feel while you are doing this activity. What is happening in your body? Is your heart racing? Is your skin tingling? Are you screaming for the thrill of it? Now I want you to think about what goes on in your body when you are feeling fearful. Do you notice any similarities between the sensations of excitement and the sensations of fear?

Fearless People Get Up After They Fall

Michael Jordan is considered one of the greatest basketball players of all time. In his basketball career, he won five MVP awards, appeared in fourteen NBA All Star Games, and won too many titles and awards to list.

But you probably expected all of that. Here's something that most people don't know about Michael Jordan: He was cut from his high school basketball team.

Being cut from a sporting team is a huge blow to an athlete's ego. Many athletes don't come back after something like that. They associate being cut from the team as a sign that they are no good and then give up.

But Michael Jordan obviously didn't give up. He refused to believe that it was not possible for him to become a great ball player. In order to make the team, he practiced for hours on the court. He was quoted as saying, "Whenever I was working out and got tired and figured I ought to stop, I'd close my eyes and see that list in the locker room without my name on it, and that usually got me going again."

He not only eventually made the team, he eventually led it to a state championship.

Here's something else you might not know about Jordan. During his professional basketball career, he missed 9,000 shots. He also lost 300 games. And 26 times the ball was passed to him just before the game's end—giving him the opportunity to win for the team—and he missed the shot.

As he said in a Nike commercial, "I've failed over and over in my life, and that is why I succeed."

Jordan's story beautifully shows how fearless people view failure differently than fearful people do. He and other fearless people do not see failure as a flaw, as cause for embarrassment, or as an indictment of who they are as people. Simply put, it doesn't define them.

BE FEARLESS: *Failing at something doesn't make you a failure.*

And they definitely don't see it as a sign that their dreams are impossible.

No, they just see failure as an opportunity to learn, grow, and become even better.

Just in case you are shaking your head and thinking that Jordan must be an anomaly, I'd like to share a few more stories about people who saw possibilities in the face of the impossible.

One of them: Babe Ruth. He's considered one of the greatest baseball players of all time. He hit 714 home runs during his career. He also struck out 1,330 times. He was quoted as saying, "Every strike brings me closer to the next home run."

But it's not just athletes who fail and try again. So do entrepreneurs. Henry Ford failed over and over again—completely going broke five times—before he founded the Ford Motor Company. R. H. Macy started seven businesses that failed before he finally founded the department store that still bears his name. Walt Disney was once fired from his job as a newspaper editor and told that he "lacked imagination." Many great scientists—including Isaac Newton and Albert Einstein—did not perform well in school. Thomas Edison made a thousand lightbulbs that didn't work before he finally made one that did. Oprah Winfrey was fired from her first job as a television reporter and was told she was "unfit for TV."

And Vincent van Gogh only sold one painting during his lifetime. His artwork now sells for millions and is among the most expensive and coveted in the world.

Now, it's important to understand that fearless people don't fail and try again blindly. If they did that, they would never become successful. No, they fail and use that failure as an opportunity, one that:

- Helps them reassess what they are doing right and what they are doing wrong.
- Provides insight into which parts of their plan are working and which parts aren't.
- Motivates them to try even harder.
- Encourages them to tap into resources and support.
- Spurs them to reinvent themselves.

Think About It

Only you can determine whether a dream or a goal is possible or impossible for you. How strong is your passion? Do you believe in it? Who determines your fate—you or others? Are you satisfied with the status quo?

If you are reeling from a past failure, use this advice to find the courage to make a comeback:

- **Change your thinking.** Switch from *Everyone thinks I'm a failure* to *This is a great opportunity for me to grow.*
- **Be smart.** Research the situation. Be well informed about strategies you can use in the future so you can learn from and avoid mistakes you've made in the past.
- **Think about what you did right.** Not everything was a mistake. Build on your successes and on your strengths.
- **Create realistic goals.** Make sure they conform to the guidelines in Step 1 of the program.

Fearless People Don't Personalize Rejection

I'd like to tell you a story about my personal journey with my advice column. It already ran in New York, Boston, and Philadelphia, but I wanted to expand my reach. I started pitching myself to other very large metropolitan newspapers like the *New York Times*, the *Washington Post*, and the *Chicago Tribune*. I also pitched myself to national magazines like *Ladies' Home Journal*, *Men's Health*, and *Cosmopolitan*.

I pitched myself. I got rejected. I pitched myself. I got rejected. I pitched myself. I got rejected.

I could have interpreted all of those rejections like this: *I should just be happy with the column that I have. I already reach a million readers. I'm lucky I at least have that. I should just give up. Nobody is going to hire me. I was so bad at writing in junior high that the teacher called my parents and scheduled an intervention. That should have taught me a lesson. I'm a terrible writer.*

I didn't. In fact, it never even occurred to me to personalize it. The rejection didn't bother me, in part, because I expected it. In overcoming my fear of approaching women, I had already learned this important life lesson: To get just one acceptance, I must approach many.

BE FEARLESS: *Expect rejection. Pitch a hundred, land one.*

I told myself, *I can deal with rejection. This is what it takes. I might have to pitch eighty newspapers. It doesn't matter if seventy-nine of them say no, as long as one of them says yes.* I knew that it took many, many nos before I would get to yes. I knew that getting rejected was no big deal. It was a necessary part of the journey. I expected it actually.

The rejection also didn't bother me for another reason. It's this: I didn't take it personally. A fearful person might get rejected and personalize it, telling him- or herself, *I'm no good. I can't even put together something that they like.*

I assumed they turned me down not because they didn't want me or because they thought I wasn't good enough. To the contrary, I assumed they turned me down because they lacked the space for a new column, didn't have the budget for one, or some other reason. I knew that one rejection didn't make me a reject. Neither did ten rejections or even one hundred. Rejection didn't define me.

The only way I would be a reject would be if I didn't try at all.

I didn't just expect rejection; I also embraced it and learned from it. One day between clients, I called in to retrieve my voice mail. There was a message from a syndication service I had pitched. The editor told me he was rejecting my column and why. "You have to get to the advice faster," he said. "I am reading what you submitted to us and I'm just thinking, where is the fucking advice?"

Yes, the words stung, and, yes, there was no reason for him to be so rough. Still, I used it as a learning opportunity. I realized my sample column had to be more hard-hitting, specific, and advice oriented. I rewrote it and sent out some more. From that point on readers got their advice sooner.

BE FEARLESS: *You are bigger and stronger than just one rejection.*

Next on my pitch list was the *Los Angeles Times*. I looked on the masthead and I called the managing editor. I got voice mail. I called again and left another message. I called and I called. One day she happened to answer her phone. I pitched the column idea. She said, "You know, you are not supposed to be calling someone as high up as me. You could have just sent an e-mail."

I said, "I'd rather be rejected to my face than to not hear anything back at all. And anyway, we're talking now. I have your attention." We discussed the paper's needs and how my expertise might be utilized. She was impressed. She gave me the column, and it was well received.

I could just as easily have been rejected that day. It still wouldn't have caused me to feel like a reject. I would have used each rejection as a chance to improve my delivery so I could try again. While fearless people accept and even embrace rejection as a necessary part of life, fearful people don't. They tend to collect rejections and see them as signs that they are no good. For them, each rejection becomes a negative reference experience (see page 27 for more on reference experiences). The negative reference experiences start to define them and become meshed with their sense of self. For the fearful, every rejection becomes evidence that they are no good, incapable, not good enough, and a loser. "Why bother trying?" the fearful person asks. "I'm just going to screw it up." In this way, they become negative experience collectors. Each rejection, criticism, difficulty, or unexpected result causes them to feel like a failure and like their dreams are impossible. As a result their self-confidence drops and they become anxious and depressed, which renders them unable to fulfill their dreams.

The fearless, on the other hand, grow stronger and bolder with each rejection. Yes, the rejection stings, but it doesn't make them feel like a reject and it doesn't stop them from trying even harder.

Think About It

Do you brace for rejection? Does each *no* cause you to feel like a failure? *No* doesn't always mean no. It might just mean that you need to find a new way to approach a person or a situation. How can you learn from the rejection in your life? How can you use it to fine-tune your approach, reinvent yourself, or create a new opportunity?

To stay confident in the face of rejection, use these tips:

• **Expect to be rejected.** Rather than formulate ways to avoid rejection, consider that rejection is a part of life and a necessary part of success. The more people you proposition, the greater your chances of getting rejected and the greater your chances of getting a yes, too. Proposition many to land one.

- **Know that rejection is the only way to get to acceptance.** If you don't try at all, you definitely won't get what you want.
- **Believe that you are stronger than the rejection.** Think of your past rejections. How bad were they in reality?
- **Remember: it's not about you!** It doesn't mean that you are a bad or an unlovable person. It only means that you were not the right match for this job, person, or opportunity.
- **Use each rejection as a learning opportunity.** Can you change your strategy? Can you change your goals? Is there a different route to the same destination?

Fearless People Find Certainty in the Midst of Uncertainty

As I've mentioned earlier, fear is about uncertainty. It's about not being able to predict what will happen next. This unpredictability breeds anxiety.

And in the midst of uncertainty, fearless people react very differently than fearful ones do. Take the ups and downs of the stock market as an example. When I was working on this book, the stock market in the United States was extremely volatile. Three countries were on the verge of defaulting on their debts, and the U.S. economy was in bad shape. As a result, the Dow Jones Industrial Average frequently would tumble 300, 400, 500, or more points a day.

Many people understandably found this quite scary. After all, the volatility made predicting the market nearly impossible. People worried: Will stocks tumble even more? Will I lose my life savings?

Will the United States go back into recession? Is this a sign of another Great Depression?

What I found interesting was how differently some people reacted to the stock market's volatility than others. Fearful people generally had one of two reactions. One was a form of denial. They asked people not to talk about the stock market because they found the news too "anxiety provoking." They essentially put their hands over their eyes and their heads in the sand. Other fearful people did the opposite. They tended to gossip about it. They posted updates on Facebook about it and then nervously talked to friends about it.

Fearless people, however, did something different. They didn't jump to conclusions or panic. Instead they read reliable financial news, they called their brokers, and they compiled statistics. They looked at the big picture. They learned as much as they could about the world economy and the stock market in general. This information allowed them to create some certainty in the midst of an uncertain situation.

It's the same with any type of uncertainty. For example, whenever I see clients who are afraid of flying, I get them to learn as much as they can about the mechanics of flying. The more they know, the more they understand and the less uncertain they feel. Health problems are the same. The more you can learn about a possible diagnosis, the less uncertain you will feel and the less fear you will have.

Think About It

How do you react to uncertainty? Do you react by being a good researcher and trying to find out what you need to know so you can make better predictions? Or do you react by putting your hands over your ears or by gossiping and spreading rumors?

Fearless People Practice Being Fearless

On January 15, 2009, US Airways Flight 1549 out of New York encountered a flock of birds ninety seconds after takeoff. Pilot C. B. "Sully" Sullenberger had no time to take evasive action. Soon the plane rocked, and Sully could hear loud thuds as the birds were being sucked into the engines. And then there was silence. Both engines failed. Sullenberger knew he could not coast a powerless aircraft back to the airport, so he attempted to put the plane down in the one place where there would be the fewest ground casualties—the Hudson River. As you might remember, he was able to land the plane in one piece, and all 155 people on board survived.

When many people heard this news story, I'm pretty sure they wondered, *How the heck did he stop himself from freaking out as the plane was going down?*

I'm sure Sullenberger was freaked out to some degree. Of course he felt some nerves. He was quoted as saying that the moments before the crash were, "the worst sickening, pit-of-your-stomach, falling-through-the-floor feeling." If he didn't experience such sensations, he wouldn't be human. As I've already explained, however, he probably interpreted those sensations much differently than a fearful person would interpret them. As you've learned, the fear response can actually be quite helpful during a life-threatening situation. Sullenberger's was. It gave him exactly what he needed in that moment: more strength, better eyesight, and the ability to think and react quickly.

But Sullenberger probably didn't freak out for at least another reason. It's this: he was a highly experienced pilot, one who had flown for more than forty years and who had accrued nineteen thousand hours of flying. He'd flown F-14 fighter jets for the Navy, and he had investigated aircraft accidents. He knew what to do, and he did it.

You may not be able to safely land a huge airplane on the Hudson River or even on a runway without freaking out, but that's because you haven't practiced or trained to perform such a feat.

Similarly, you may not feel comfortable running into a burning building to save a child or even a dog or cat. A firefighter, on the other hand, does feel comfortable doing so, and that's because the firefighter has trained to do this very thing.

My brother, Matthew, is a police officer in Washington, D.C. He is assigned to the Capitol, one of the most important buildings in the country. On September 11, 2001, when people were fleeing Washington, D.C., in a panic, Matthew was heading *into* Washington to do whatever he could do to help. It was his call to duty, and he didn't even think twice about it. He's trained to protect and keep order. It's what he knows how to do.

As you can see from these stories, fear loses its power when you prepare yourself to meet it head-on. If you walked out onto a stage without preparing for a speech, of course you would be scared! But if you walk onto a stage after preparing—practicing your lines and learning your craft—the fear won't be quite as strong.

And that's exactly what the BE FEARLESS five-step plan does. It teaches you how to break what, at the moment, might seem like a huge, unattainable goal down into smaller mini-goals that will allow you to practice a skill over and over again until you feel more confident. And, eventually, by practicing being fearless over and over again, it will become second nature to you.

Think About It

What in your life do you least fear and why? Have you forgotten what you've mastered? Think about all of the things you do every day and don't even have to think about because you are already an expert at them. It might be riding a bike, catching a baseball, or even cooking a gourmet dinner. Some people find these activities scary because they have not mastered them yet. But you have. You can master more skills too.

Fearless People Think About What's Possible

In the early 1950s, many people believed that it was impossible for humans to run a mile in under four minutes. After all, runners had been trying to break the four-minute barrier since the late 1800s. The world's top coaches and most gifted athletes had been trying to go "sub-4.0" for years. They were dedicated, and they'd tried all sorts of training plans.

Yet it seemed the four-minute barrier was beyond reach. People had tried to break it for so long that many were starting to believe it was impossible—that the human body just could not go that fast.

Then in 1954 Roger Bannister, a twenty-five-year-old, full-time medical student, ran the mile in 3 minutes and 59.4 seconds.

A month and a half later, John Landy ran even faster. Then a year later, three more runners broke the four-minute barrier. Today high school runners break the barrier routinely. Hicham El Guerrouj of Morocco holds the record of the world's fastest mile at 3 minutes and 43.13 seconds.

Yet people thought it was impossible. More important, once Bannister's time proved to other runners that it really and truly was possible, they were able to make the impossible possible and run the distance in under four minutes too.

Your beliefs are powerful. If you believe something is impossible, that belief will erode your confidence and turn that impossible belief into a self-fulfilling prophecy. If a person with authority—whether it's a doctor, a therapist, or a teacher—tells you that you can't do something, you will believe it, even if that person's prediction isn't accurate. And once you believe it, you will behave as if that prediction is true, by default making it come true. For instance, if I told a client, "You are really screwed up. There's no hope for you," it could cause the client to stop trying, even though there really is hope.

Just the same, positive beliefs are just as powerful. If you believe you can and will do something, you will find the means to make the impossible possible.

BE FEARLESS: *Your dream is only as impossible or possible as you believe it to be. Think what's possible and you'll make the impossible possible.*

Imagine how the world would be if President John F. Kennedy believed that it was impossible to put a man on the moon. What if Martin Luther King Jr. had believed it was impossible to achieve civil rights in the United States, or if Gandhi had believed it was impossible to overthrow the British occupation of India without violence? Could Barack Obama have become the first African-American president of the United States if he'd thought the quest was impossible? Probably not.

Believing that something is possible is the first step to making that belief come true. The second step, though, is having a vision and a plan. Fearless people don't stop at believing that the impossible can be possible. They take it further and create a plan that gets them there.

For instance, several years ago, I had never before appeared on national television. Still, being able to reach people through national media was a dream of mine, one that I refused to believe was impossible. I knew I had something important to say and advice that people could benefit from hearing. I had a clear vision of where I wanted to go and how I was going to get myself there. I defined what I wanted to accomplish, I set a timeline for getting it done, and I broke what initially seemed like a huge and daunting goal down into small minigoals. I anticipated and dealt with obstacles along the way. And I rolled with the problems as they came up.

This is exactly the same process other successful people have followed to get to where they are today. Barack Obama had a vision of how to win the election for U.S. president. He had to define his specific goal, set a timeline, rally support strategically and geographically, keep his eye on the end goal, and anticipate obstacles such as opposing views, rumors, past voting history, and so on. Finally, he needed to be flexible and confident enough to continue pursuing his goal despite any resistance and veering off course.

The BE FEARLESS five-step plan will help you to do all of this and more, so you can make the impossible possible in your life too.

Change Your Life Now!

Fearlessness is a state of mind, not a genetic trait. You can acquire it and strengthen it. Start to build your courage now by reminding yourself of all of the amazing feats you've already accomplished in your life. Chances are you have probably already made the impossible possible several times in your life. What have you already accomplished that you once thought could never be done? Write it down. Keep this list handy and read it whenever you are tempted to believe that you don't have what it takes to make changes stick.

PART TWO

The BE FEARLESS
Program

How You Will Change Your Life in 28 Days

The **BE FEARLESS** program includes one preparatory chapter followed by five powerful steps. Depending on your level of dedication, you can finish the program in as few as 28 days. Here's a preview.

. . . .

PREP:
LAY THE BE FEARLESS FOUNDATION

How It Will Change Your Life: You'll believe change really is possible, and you will be able to anticipate, plan for, and overcome obstacles that have held you back in the past.

Tasks

☐ **1.** Find a notebook that you will use to jot down notes as you progress through the program.

☐ **2.** Test your Fearless Potential by seeing where you are on the Fearless Scale.

☐ **3.** Take a quick quiz to determine whether you have Fearmongers in your life and take simple but effective steps to distance yourself from them.

☐ **4.** Ponder how television, news, gossip, and social media affect your fear and take steps to cut back if needed.

☐ **5.** Designate at least one person you can lean on for emotional support.

Estimated time to completion: 1 to 2 hours.

STEP 1:
DEFINE YOUR DREAM LIFE

How It Will Change Your Life: You'll have the passion, energy, and motivation to pursue what you've always wanted. Your dreams will no longer seem impossible. To the contrary, they will seem quite possible and within reach.

Exercises

☐ **1.** Visualize the future you want for yourself.

☐ **2.** Write a list of goals and dreams based on that visualization.

☐ **3.** Fine-tune your list by checking to make sure each goal or dream is internally motivated, appropriate, realistic, inspiring, positive, and specific.

☐ **4.** Create a Payoff List of benefits to continually move you forward.

☐ **5.** Prioritize your Dream List and pick one goal to accomplish in the next 28 days.

Estimated time to completion: 2 to 3 hours.

· ·

STEP 2:
BREAK YOUR FEAR PATTERN

How It Will Change Your Life: You will no longer fear change. You will understand what has stood between you and reaching your goals in the past and you will know how to overcome it.

Exercises

☐ **1.** Complete a Fear Dump—listing all of the worries, excuses, and concerns you have about trying to make your dream come true.

☐ **2.** Identify your Dream Stoppers—habitual emotional obstacles that have kept you from moving forward.

☐ **3.** Examine your Fear Dump to learn how your thinking keeps you stuck, and create a Stuck List based on your results.

☐ **4.** Strengthen the Payoff List you created in Step 1, using your Fear Dump and Stuck List as a guide.

Estimated time to completion: Less than 2 hours.

STEP 3:
REWRITE YOUR INNER NARRATIVE

How It Will Change Your Life: You will break out of the negativity that has held you back, led to fear, and caused you to doubt yourself in the past. You will know what to tell yourself so you can end worry, stay calm, and remain confident about your goals.

Exercises

☐ **1.** Notice your thoughts and become more aware of your negativity.

☐ **2.** Do periodic body scans to gain more insight into your feelings and sensations.

☐ **3.** Pay attention to what you say and what others say to you. Notice how language affects decisions, choices, emotions, and fear.

☐ **4.** Transcribe your mental narrative by thinking about your goal and seeing what negative thoughts bubble to the surface.

☐ **5.** Rewrite your mental narrative to make it more positive and motivating. Memorize it.

Estimated time to completion: 2 to 3 hours over the course of a week.

....

STEP 4:
ELIMINATE YOUR FEAR RESPONSE

How It Will Change Your Life: You will no longer fear anxiety, nervousness, or panic. You will be in control of your nerves. You will know what to do when you feel a racing heartbeat, sweaty palms, or another nervous sensation—and you will be able to use that response to your advantage.

Exercises

☐ **1.** Normalize your fear response by proving to yourself that no one is immune to nerves. Everyone feels them.

☐ **2.** Prove you have control over your fear response by purposely getting yourself as anxious as possible.

☐ **3.** Gain control over your fear response by calming yourself back down and practicing a relaxation exercise on a regular basis.

☐ **4.** Turn fear into a strength by discovering ways to use nerves to your advantage.

☐ **5.** Create a Fear Response Strategy to use whenever you find yourself in a tense situation.

☐ **6.** Take steps to reduce stress in your life so your fear response is less likely to kick in when you don't need it.

Estimated time to completion: 3 to 4 hours, completed over a week's time.

. . . .

STEP 5:
LIVE YOUR DREAM

How It Will Change Your Life: You will go for and reach an important life goal or dream, proving to yourself that you really can turn your dreams into a reality.

Exercises

☐ **1.** Craft a Fearless Action Plan that will help you reach your goal, one small action at a time.

☐ **2.** Embark on your Action Plan.

Estimated time to completion: This varies based on the size of the goal. You can see results in as soon as 2 weeks or as long as a few months.

Chapter Five

Lay the BE FEARLESS Foundation

The BE FEARLESS plan will help you to accomplish what you once thought was impossible. It encourages you to dare to become exceptional, face what you most fear, and overcome that invisible barrier that, until now, has been holding you back from your ultimate life.

It doesn't matter if you picked up this book because you want to overcome a fear of public speaking or a fear of failure. It doesn't matter if you want to find the courage to end a dead-end relationship or get out of a dead-end career. It doesn't matter if you have a debilitating phobia, panic disorder, or just a nagging sense that your life isn't all it could be. This plan will work for any type of fear that you might have. No fear is too big, too overwhelming, or too ingrained.

The BE FEARLESS program walks you through the same

process I use with my clients. It will take you from fearful to fearless so you can finally make your dreams come true.

With this plan, you will accomplish a lot of change in a short period of time. Change is scary. As a result you might feel a little anxious as you embark on this journey. You might have thoughts like, *Am I really ready to do this? Is now the right time for me to embark on a program of change? Do I really have what it takes?* I see this a lot with my clients. Such questions might be leading to a sense of uncertainty, and that sense of uncertainty might be causing a bit of fear. That's okay. You can do this. Any anxiety that you may be feeling right now is completely normal and expected.

I created the preparation tasks in this chapter to help you overcome these very types of jitters. These tasks will help to reduce your sense of uncertainty so you feel better prepared and more confident about the five steps that lie ahead.

These preparatory tasks will also help you to anticipate, plan for, and overcome various challenges. Although none of these prep tasks are 100 percent required, I highly encourage you to read and consider all of them so you can know that what you are about to attempt really is possible.

Change Your Life in Three Hours!

Block off one and a half to three hours to complete five preparatory tasks. Check them off as you progress.

☐ **Task #1:** Designate a notebook to use for your BE FEARLESS exercises. **Estimated time:** 1 to 30 minutes.

☐ **Task #2:** Test your Fearless Potential. Write down the date and where you are on the Fearless Scale (Stage 1 through 5) in your Fearless Notebook. **Estimated time:** 15 to 30 minutes.

☐ **Task #3:** Take the quiz to determine whether Fearmongers are in your life. Know how you will distance yourself from them. **Estimated time:** 40 to 60 minutes.

☐ **Task #4:** Read prep task #4 and consider cutting back on fear-inducing media. **Estimated time:** 15 to 30 minutes.

☐ **Task #5:** Ask at least one person to be a member of your Fearless Support Team. Write the name and contact information of your team member(s) in your Notebook. **Estimated time:** 5 to 10 minutes.

The Rules of the BE FEARLESS Program

Before diving into the prep tasks, let's go over some ground rules. Keep the following rules in mind so you can make the most of the program.

1. **There are no rules.** I've laid out this program in a way that I believe most people will be able to understand and follow. That said, there are always exceptions. If a particular exercise or step has no bearing or significance to the overriding problem or goal that you want to tackle, then by all means skip it. Beware of mental softness, though. Are you tempted to skip a step or an exercise because it scares you? Is your aversion more about your own fear and discomfort than it is about what you really need? When in doubt, do an exercise anyway, even if you don't think you will need it.

2. **If something doesn't work the first time, try it again.** I tried to create a program that is failproof. That said, life and circumstances can, at times, conspire to prevent you

from successfully completing a given exercise. When that happens, do not make the mistake of calling yourself a failure and giving up. Whenever you feel stuck, try to step outside of yourself. Think of how a friend might view the situation. How would the most confident and determined person you know tackle the problem you are having? How might that person deal with the step you are having trouble with? What would that person do differently? Also know that you might just need a short break from the program to regroup, get some perspective, and hit that mental reset button. Then when you come back to it, you might have the new perspective that you need to plow ahead.

3. **If you find yourself procrastinating, read it as a sign.** Procrastination is about fear. If you keep putting off an exercise, that means you probably need to do that exercise more than any other exercise in the book. Remember: too much thinking is what usually messes most of us up. It's overthinking that causes us to dream up excuses. Now is the time to spring into action. Stop thinking and start doing.

4. **Do each exercise for you, and not for me.** If you find yourself muttering, "I can't believe I have to do this" and "I'm supposed to do this," take a step back. No one is forcing you to become fearless. Replace those phrases with "I choose to," "I want to," "I can," and "I will."

5. **Motivate yourself by looking ahead.** Reduce frustration, stress, and fear by practicing the art of thinking forward. Keep the end result in mind at all times. Inspire yourself by keeping your mind on all that you are about to achieve.

6. **Keep an open mind.** You might find some of the exercises in this plan completely counterintuitive. For instance, very soon, I will be giving you this paradoxical prescription:

get as anxious as you possibly can. I ask you to trust me. Often what we think will never work is actually what we need to move forward. I've counseled countless people. These paradoxical exercises have worked on client after client after client. These clients, at times, initially looked at me as if they thought I was the one who needed help. Eventually, however, they all thanked me.

Prep Task #1: Get a Notebook

This plan is simple and inexpensive. You don't need much to get started, but one valuable tool I highly recommend you get is a notebook. You'll use it to take notes on your progress as you navigate the program.

Now, don't look at writing in your notebook as a "dear diary" style exercise. If you use it for listing all of your complaints about yourself and the world, then you will be reducing the notebook to nothing more than a bad therapist, the kind that makes you feel powerless instead of powerful. I'm not asking you to buy a notebook so you can write page after page about what is wrong with your life and whose fault that is. This isn't the place to complain about your boss, your friends, your mother, your past, your spouse, or your overall life. It's not for ranting and it's not for stream-of-consciousness daydreaming.

No, I want you to use your notebook for a much smarter reason. I want your notebook to become a strategic tool that you can use to help you grow in your fearlessness.

It doesn't matter what your notebook looks like. It can be fancy and expensive, or it can be plain and inexpensive. It is, however, important for your notebook to contain paper. I would prefer that you did not use an electronic notebook. Many of my clients ask me if they can just take notes on their laptops or smartphones. I always encourage them to handwrite. I do this because I've found that my clients who take handwritten notes tend to be more committed and reach success more quickly than clients who use electronic devices for note taking. This is likely due to handwriting stimulating an area of the brain associated with focus and attention. Writing down notes or goals on paper instead of typing them onto a screen helps you remember them and prioritize them. Various studies have also shown that children and adults tend to learn more quickly when they handwrite information instead of typing it. Finally, having your notes on paper—where you can see them—provides more accountability. It's more tangible because you can see and touch your notebook. It's also easier for you to organize information because you can see the beginning, middle, and end of the journey, making a paper notebook much more inspiring and motivating than an electronic one.

Throughout the program, I'll be referring to this notebook as your Fearless Notebook. I'll be suggesting specific notes for you to jot down in it and specific exercises for you to work through with pen and paper. Here are some more notes you may wish to keep:

- Motivating sayings that you come across and would like to remember.
- A periodic ranking of your fear, mood, and happiness. For instance, once a week you might rank your happiness on a scale of 1 (so sad you don't want to get out of bed) to 10 (beyond euphoric).
- A tally of your negative and positive fear experiences as you navigate the program. As I mentioned earlier, our negativity bias causes us to remember negative events over positive ones. This tally will help you to see and remember the many times a day when you are able to triumph over your fear.

Prep Task #2: Test Your Fearless Potential

Do you worry that you don't have what it takes to BE FEARLESS? It's my firm belief that you do. You are ready and able. You bought the book. That was when your decision was made. You are already curious, and curiosity leads to change. Be courageous. Look forward to the changes. Get excited. Think positive. And even if you are struggling, know that I will teach you exactly how to think positive and accomplish your dreams and goals in the coming pages.

I haven't met a single person who couldn't achieve change. That's how I know you can do it too. I wouldn't steer you wrong. I know what I am doing. Trust me on this.

But you want more than my word. Of course you do. That's why I've included the following test of your Fearless Potential. This short, simple test will prove to you that you are already more fearless than you think. More important, it will show you that you have the potential—as all people do—to become even more fearless. It's based on an adaptation of Abraham Maslow's model of learning called "the four stages of competence," and James O. Prochaska's and Carlo DiClemente's model of change called "the stages of change."

How to Test Your Fearless Potential

Read each stage of the Fearless Scale, starting with Stage 1. Answer the corresponding questions and continue from stage to stage until you find the stage you are currently in.

The Fearless Scale

Stage 1: Blind Uncertainty

What it is: In this stage, you don't even realize that you have a problem. You have no intention of changing your life because you don't know that learning or changing could do you any good. You not only don't realize that fear is the source of your problems, you also are not aware that you have a problem or could even benefit from change. Think of fearful people you know who don't even realize they are fearful. They might tell you that they are just "careful" or "realistic" when they refuse to fly, attempt change, or something else. That's blind uncertainty.

Answer this question: Did you buy this book for yourself?

If you answered yes: You are not in Stage 1. Since you've already purchased this book and have read this far, I can tell you with great certainty that you've already advanced beyond this stage. Congratulations! Move on to Stage 2.

If you answered no: You might be in Stage 1 if you are only reading this book because someone in your life—a spouse, a friend, or a colleague—suggested you read it. If so, go back and reread chapters 1 through 4.

Stage 2: Uncomfortable Uncertainty

What it is: In this stage you have become enlightened about the problem and the source of your fear. You know you are unfulfilled and what you ought to do to change that situation. Yet your current level of discomfort is still outweighed by your fear. There are some factors about your current situation that you like and don't want to give up. You think your life might get better if you make a change, but you worry that it might just as easily get worse. Think of the smoker who wakes with a really bad cough, knows it's from the smoking, and thinks, *I really ought to stop doing this.* Then the smoker starts to feel withdrawal symptoms setting in. Those symptoms aren't pleasant. To avoid feeling the pain, the smoker pulls out a cigarette so he can move back into a place of comfort. That's uncomfortable uncertainty.

Answer this question: Are you so uncomfortable right now that you're pretty sure that any change must be better than staying stuck?

If you answered yes: You are already past Stage 2. See? I told you that you were more fearless than you thought. Move on to Stage 3.

If you answered no: Realize the process of facing your fear brings up temporary discomfort. This discomfort eventually goes away once you make change stick. Doing nothing, on the other hand, will result in more of the same—permanent discomfort. Think about this for a while until you come to the firm conclusion that temporary discomfort is much better than permanent discomfort. Once you believe this and answer the above question in the affirmative, move on to Stage 3. Remember: short-term stress is better than long-term misery.

Stage 3: The Uncertainty Threshold

What it is: In this stage the discomfort of staying the same has outweighed the discomfort of change. It's quite obvious to you that doing something will be better than doing nothing. Now you are motivated to change, and you are taking small steps toward that change.

Answer this question: Have you already tried to overcome your fear? For instance, maybe you've been seeing a therapist, you've read other books, or you've tried other approaches.

If you answered yes: You are already past Stage 3! Move on to Stage 4.

If you answered no: Stage 3 is a great stage for you to be in as you attempt this program. If you are in Stage 3, you are ready for change. The five-step program will move forward at precisely the right pace for you. Although you may feel a little uncomfortable at any given time, you will never feel completely overwhelmed. By the time you finish the program, you will have naturally progressed to or beyond Stage 4.

Stage 4: Cautious Certainty

What it is: In this stage, you are moving forward and attempting to change your life and become more fearless. Still, this is all new to you, so you feel uncomfortable, just as you probably felt when you rode a bicycle for the first time. I remember my dad teaching me how to ride a bike. As I was moving along I looked back and realized he was a hundred feet behind me and that he had let go long ago. I realized, *I'm really doing this on my own!* I had such a feeling of accomplishment. Soon you will have that feeling of accomplishment too. Right now, however, you're not completely comfortable riding that bike on your own.

Answer this question: Have you faced what you most fear and found out that it wasn't quite as scary as you thought it would be?

If you answered yes: Wow, you're more fearless than you ever thought! You must be in Stage 5. Beware of being overly confident though. This is the stage of any fearless journey where many people run into problems. Dieters lose weight and then gain it back. People walk away from dead-end relationships only to return to them. What's happening in these cases is that folks are relapsing and returning to an earlier stage on the fearless continuum. Usually they are relapsing because they haven't taken steps to strengthen their fearlessness and turn it into a lifestyle. That's what chapter 11 in this book helps you to do. There you will find what you need to know to make your changes stick so you can prevent relapse and embark on a lifelong journey into fearlessness.

If you answered no: You are normal. No, I take that back. You are exceptional. You are already in Stage 4, whereas most people don't get to this stage until they've completed the five steps. Feel good about where you are on the Fearless Scale, and know that life only gets better from here. The five-step plan will help you strengthen your fearlessness even more so you can go on to achieve all of your dreams—even the ones that, right now, might seem impossible.

Stage 5: Master of Certainty

What it is: This is the end of the line—the stage when you realize that maintaining your changes is no longer a struggle and you have no temptation to regress to your old dysfunctional habits. Your fearless thoughts and behaviors are now automated. Going after your goals and dreams feels almost effortless.

This is the stage where you will be once you finish this book. Thoughts and behaviors that feel foreign and awkward to you now will eventually feel second nature and effortless as you reach your goals.

By the end of this book you will answer this question with a strong yes! Do you make a lifestyle out of confronting your fear?

You probably won't answer this yes now, but you will agree with that statement soon. I encourage you to revisit this scale once you complete the five steps and again after to accomplish one dream after another.

Prep Task #3: Distance Yourself from Fearmongers

A Fearmonger is someone who either consciously or unconsciously causes fear to spread.

Simply put, they're negative. They could win the lottery and find something to complain about. They could have the day off from work and complain or even get promoted and complain. They complain about everything and anything, including their jobs, other friends, family, relatives, the government, celebrities, gas prices, the stock market, heck, even the weather.

It's taxing to be around them. Fearmongers can suck the energy right out of you. Life is often filled with drama or even a series of crises for these people.

Rarely will a Fearmonger truly take an interest in you, ask about your goals and dreams, or offer anything encouraging. They can be self-absorbed, demanding, have a victim mentality, and lack empathy.

Worst of all: they cause fear to spread, and this can be quite destructive for you right now.

I'm guessing you probably have one or more Fearmongers in your life. Sometimes Fearmongers are difficult to spot because we've become so accustomed to them and have, in a way, come to accept them for how they are. How many times have you thought or said, "Oh, she's just a tough one" or "He's just negative, that's all." That may be true, and that may have been acceptable in the past. Now, however, you're making big positive changes in your life. It's important to recognize the negative impact that Fearmongers like this could have on you.

I often give my clients this analogy so they can better understand the impact that people's opinions—positive or negative—might have on them. Let's say you've decided to buy a new Toyota Prius. You are feeling confident about this decision and you can't wait to sign on the dotted line. You excitedly tell your brother about the car and he says, "A Prius? That car looks like a sneaker with tires." Now you are feeling a little doubt. It looks like a sneaker? Really? So you call a friend and you tell her that you are thinking about buying a Prius. You say, "Can you believe my brother told me that it looks like a giant sneaker?" She says, "Well, it kinda does." Now you've got even more doubt. So you ask your mother about it. She responds, "You're getting a Prius? Why would you buy a car like that?" Now your confidence is shaken and your belief system has begun to change.

Fearmongers create uncertainty, promote negativity, and shake your confidence. Right now you are trying to strengthen your belief in your own fearlessness. The fearmongers, though, serve to weaken that belief.

It's important to note that in therapy, I serve as the opposite of a Fearmonger. Whereas a Fearmonger works to shake and destabilize a healthy belief system, I work to shake and destabilize unhealthy beliefs and create new, healthy ones in their place. Fearmongers work to convince you to be more fearful and to do less with your life. I work to convince you and others to be more fearless and do more with your life. Fearmongers make you weaker. I, along with this program, will make you stronger.

WHO ARE YOUR FEARMONGERS?

Take a moment and think about your family of origin, your close friends, your coworkers, and your casual acquaintances. Then look at the checklist below. Put each of these people to the Fearmonger test.

Question	Answer: Yes or No
1. Is the person generally negative?	
2. Is the person unhappy in career, with family, and in relationships?	
3. Does the person complain about news, gas prices, politics, and so on?	
4. Do you feel exhausted after spending time with the person?	
5. Does the person make fun of your goals?	

continued

Question	Answer: Yes or No
6. Do you feel discouraged after spending time with the person?	
7. Is the person demanding?	
8. Is the person self-absorbed?	
9. Is there a lot of drama or crisis in the person's life?	
10. Does the person often have a helpless or victim mentality?	

If you answered yes to more than three questions, then this person is probably a Fearmonger and isn't going to help you reach your goals and dreams. You might think that three out of ten affirmative answers isn't that bad. Don't overlook the negativity bias. It only takes a little negativity to weaken your resolve. Think of it this way: if someone you know is negative 30 percent of the time, that means this person inserts fear into your life for approximately eighteen minutes of every hour, nearly eight hours of every day, and two or three days out of every week. That can really add up!

WHAT TO DO ABOUT FEARMONGERS

Depending on your life and circumstances, you might not be able to avoid all of the Fearmongers in your life. But you can do the following.

- **Keep your distance and maintain your boundaries.** Now's the time to put your needs first and foremost. Stay focused on your goal and your dream. Realize that your goals are more important than a nagging and negative friend. A true friend will understand and respect you and your goals.

- **Don't stoop to their level.** Until now, you've probably played a role in the spread of fear. Think about the role you've played. Does a certain friend or group of friends come to you just to gossip because they know you will join in? If so, how can you use your words to defuse fear? How might you interrupt the fear-spreading cycle? Rather than one-upping your friend's fear gossip, for instance, could you sit back, listen, and respond with a more positive statement like, "Oh I'm sure everything will be okay"?

- **Don't rescue them.** To do so only enables their behavior and drains you.

- **Don't feel obligated to remain close.** Know that people change over time. Case in point: I don't feel obligated to be friends with people just because I knew them back in high school. As a matter of fact, I remain close to just one friend, Dave, whom I've known since kindergarten. I remain friends with him because I want to, but not because I feel I have to. If the person's goals, beliefs, and values are in line with yours, then go for it. If not, then phase them out.

- **Be strong and stand up for yourself.** To appear vulnerable only provides an opportunity for the toxic friend to continue to suck the life out of you.

- **Speak up and be proud of your goals.** Remember, you're doing something healthy!

- **Create cooling-off periods.** When Fearmongers call, let it go to voice mail. That way you can check the message and gauge where a person is emotionally before engaging with that person. If the message is very anxious and fear based, you might wait a few hours before returning the call. The time lapse might allow the Fearmonger a chance to move on to another topic.

Prep Task #4: Inoculate Yourself Against Fear

If you were about to go on a diet, you would probably take some steps to reduce your temptation for certain foods. For instance, you might get cookies and chips out of the house. Or you might hide them by putting them in opaque containers and up high in a cabinet you don't use very often. Such techniques would help you to avoid craving and temptation.

You can do the same with fear. There are many ways society works to increase our fear. We just talked about Fearmongers and how they work to trigger and worsen fear. But there are plenty of other sources.

The news, with its heavy emphasis on crime and natural disasters, tends to set people up to feel fearful. We're bombarded with negative, threatening information in a 24/7 news cycle. We can't turn on the TV or read a paper without hearing, seeing, or reading about danger. We learn about children snatched from their front yards, strange and deadly diseases that we could catch from birds, and problems associated with everything we use and come in contact with, ranging from toasters that spontaneously catch on fire to toxic mold that could be lurking in your shower stall.

No wonder we're so fearful!

There's no breathing room and no time to process. We're constantly reminded of the bad economy, job loss, and unemployment. We keep hearing about corporations and banks folding.

Added to all of that is story after story about high divorce rates, infidelity, cheating celebrities, scandals, and gruesome crimes. This all sends a negative message, instilling and perpetuating fear. Consciously or unconsciously people develop a hyper vigilance.

> ### *Test It Out*
>
> Rate your fear on a 1 to 10 scale before you watch the evening news. Then rate it again after the news is over. Does the news—with its heavy emphasis on gloom, doom, and turmoil—exacerbate your fear? Chances are that it does.

Further, although the Internet, texting, Facebook, instant messaging, status updates, and smartphones all offer incredible conveniences and efficiency, there's a drawback that is leading to more fear. If your Facebook stream or inbox is full of fearful messages about stock market fluctuations, the economy, and other scary news events, you will probably feel yourself tense up whenever you are online. There's an expectation that we should be constantly connected and accessible. This breeds uncertainty. What if we're not constantly connected? What might we miss? What will people think if we don't get back to them right away? Because of all these technological advances, there's more room for urgency and uncertainty than ever.

Even television shows and movies can bring up fear. Think about how you feel after watching a scary movie. Is that how you want to feel as you are attempting to embark on a life-changing program?

Here are some ways you might decide to put your fear on a diet:

- Avoid crime dramas, horror flicks, and apocalyptic dramas. Choose comedies and feel-good dramas instead.
- Limit your news exposure to one trusted source that goes beyond sensationalized, fear-inducing reporting.
- If you have a group of friends who make a pastime out of gossiping about fear—*Did you hear the next terrorism*

attack will be during a major sporting event?—you might want to change the subject. Take control and lead the conversation elsewhere.

- Go on Facebook and other social sites only *after* you've tackled your fearless exercises for the day.

Prep Task #5: Create a Fearless Support Team

Just as some people tend to be Fearmongers, others tend to evoke fearlessness.

Think of the people in your life who generally put you at ease and cause you to feel as if all is okay with the world. These are the people who see the glass half full more often than they see it half empty. They are the type of people who believe in you, encourage you, and generally make you feel like a rock star. For me it's my family and a reliable friend named John, who is in his late seventies. No matter what, they always see the good in me.

These are the people you want by your side. They are the very people you want to talk to when you are feeling weak because they will help you feel strong again. These are the people who would make ideal members of your Fearless Support Team.

Your support team can have as few or as many members as you'd like. To make sure each person you choose has what it takes to motivate you toward success, read the following questions. If the answer to all three questions is yes, then this person would make a great addition to your Fearless Support Team.

1. Do you admire this person's ability to embrace change?
2. Does this person motivate you to strive for something more?
3. Would you feel comfortable telling this person about your goals?

Tell each person that you are about to embark on a life-changing plan that will help you reach a very important goal. As you navigate the steps of the program, I will nudge you from time to time on ways to include your Fearless Support Team in your journey. Tell your fearless supporters about what you are trying to do and why it's so important to you. Ask them to offer advice and encouragement as needed.

Surrounding yourself with like-minded people is powerful. In addition to a Fearless Support Team, you might even suggest that a friend or a group of friends buy the book so you can all work through the program together.

Fearless Makeover

Amy, thirty-two, was about to embark on a huge life change. She had been working in human resources for the past decade and wanted to switch careers and become a labor attorney. This was an ambitious undertaking and would require her to devote a lot of time, money, and hard work to make it happen. Career changes can create a lot of fear and anxiety, and leave people feeling uncertain about whether they're making the right decision. It's vital to have full support from friends and family. Amy feared she didn't have the support she needed. In particular, there were a few people in her life who'd already voiced their discouragement.

The Goal: Amy wanted to surround herself with supportive friends and family and not be distracted by those who were negative and who instilled fear.

continued

The Payoff: If she learned how to deal with the unsupportive people in her life, Amy would be able to pursue law school and change careers with more confidence and less stress.

The Program: I helped Amy to identify her needs. Not surprisingly, achieving her law degree and having full support from friends was paramount.

I asked her to take the Fearmonger quiz (Prep Task #3) and, based on her results, make two lists: one of people who supported her dream and another of people who did not. After making these lists, it became clear who Amy could count on to help her reach her goal and who she couldn't. I then talked to Amy about people pleasing and why she felt obligated to remain friends with the people who were holding her back from her dream. I then counseled her to keep her distance from the Fearmongers.

The Outcome: Amy shifted her focus to the people in her life who were supportive and paid a lot less attention to the Fearmongers. As she got what she needed from her supportive friends, she felt far less of a need to engage with the other folks in her life. The Fearmongers had a far weaker presence in her life than before, and Amy was able to assemble a supportive team as she embarked on law school.

Chapter Six

Step 1: Define Your Dream Life

Everyone has dreams, but only a few people make those dreams a reality.

You are about to become one of the few.

To make your dreams come true, you don't need years of one-on-one consultations with the most expensive therapist in the country, and you don't necessarily need a prescription either. You don't need to listen to expensive audios designed to rewire your brain, and you also don't need to take costly supplements designed to calm the mind. All you will need are a pen or pencil, paper, and a determination to change. The only thing standing between you and what you want is this: you. It's time to get out of your own way. It's time to become fearless.

Once you finish this chapter, I can guarantee that you will not see life quite the same way as you did before you started reading. That's because you will have seen and defined your dream life. And once you've seen and defined the dream, you will finally understand how to create the life you really want.

Yes, this chapter will change you. It will fill you with the passion and energy that may have been missing from your life. It will give you that kick in the pants you need to break out of monotony and mediocrity—and to start striving toward what, until now, may have seemed impossible.

That's exciting.

But I must warn you: The initial step in this program is just as deceiving as it is exciting. It's deceiving because the exercises you will do to complete the first step of this program are not complicated or time-consuming. You may be able to whip through everything suggested in this chapter in as little as one hour.

Sounds like cake, right?

It's not. In the following pages, you will be defining your goal, what we will affectionately call your "dream." Dreaming is healthy, and pursuing a dream is even healthier. It's mobilizing. It's energizing, and it can get you out of just about any rut you might be in right now.

Still, this might bring up some fear, ranging from fear of change to fear of success. Change is stressful. In my practice I see people all the time who are getting married or buying a home. These are positive and happy events, but nonetheless they are very stressful. I even counseled a guy who had recently gotten a promotion and a big fat raise, so he'd celebrated by trading in his beat-up old Ford for a new Mercedes. This new car filled him with anxiety! It was a good change, but it was still a change, and all change is stressful.

In order to succeed, you must embrace stress as a natural side effect of change. There is no way around it. Things are going to get a little uncomfortable.

But you can do this. I'm going to be with you too. Because I've used these exercises with so many of my clients, I have anticipated where you might get stuck or even feel overwhelmed and start to retreat. I've predicted the exercises that might tempt you to back off or cause you to talk yourself out of pursuing your dream at all. Think of me as your coach, your therapist, or your motivational guru.

I even have figured out when, because of fear, you might be tempted to put this book down and walk away. In those places, you'll find that I've inserted **Fear Antidotes**. It's normal to want to avoid anticipated anxiety. Why wouldn't you try to get out of feeling uncomfortable if you could? It's human to try to maintain the status quo, but the status quo isn't always what's good for you and it doesn't always lead to happiness.

Sometimes change is the only answer, and these antidotes will help you to move past your mental resistance so you can embrace change and move toward what you really want in life.

Change Your Life in Three Hours!

Step 1 includes five exercises that will take you anywhere from two to three hours to complete. I encourage you to block off a chunk of time for these exercises and do them one after the other. They all relate to one another. Check them off as you move forward.

☐ **Exercise #1:** Visualize the future you want for yourself. See it in detail. **Estimated time:** 20 to 30 minutes.

☐ **Exercise #2:** Write a Dream List based on your visualization from Exercise #1. Don't hold anything back. **Estimated time:** 15 to 20 minutes.

☐ **Exercise #3:** Fine-tune your Dream List by checking to make sure each goal or dream is internally motivated, appropriate, realistic, inspiring, positive, and specific. **Estimated time:** 15 to 20 minutes.

continued

☐ **Exercise #4:** Create a Payoff List. Write it in your
Fearless Notebook. List all of the benefits of facing your
fear and reaching your goal. **Estimated time:** 15 to
20 minutes.

☐ **Exercise #5:** Prioritize your Dream List. Pick one goal or
dream to reach in the next 28 days. **Estimated time:** 5 to
10 minutes.

Exercise #1: See Your Future

This exercise will help you to dig deep, get honest with yourself,
and uncover what you truly want and where you really want to go.

Relax in a comfortable place, somewhere you feel safe, secure,
and free to dream. It should be a place that you do not associate
with judgment or ridicule. It should be a place that makes you feel
good, one that brings a smile to your face when you think about
it. Maybe that's a favorite room in your home. Maybe it's a park.
Maybe it's your favorite chair. Maybe it's your backyard. Or maybe
it's even a place of worship. Wherever it is, go there.

Eliminate the possibility of distractions. Turn off the computer
and phone. **Then spend some time thinking about the following questions:**

- What excites you?
- What do you love?
- What are you passionate about?
- Who do you admire and why?
- Who are your heroes and why?
- Who do you wish you were more like and why?

- Whose life would you like to have and why?
- Think about people in your life who excite you. What are they doing? Why do you find it exciting?
- Who in your life do you find inspiring? What about this person inspires you?
- If you could be someone else, who would you be?
- What is missing from your life?
- If you could be doing anything right now, what would you be doing?
- If you could be working anywhere, where would you be working?
- What would you do or have in your life if money were not an obstacle?
- What would you do if you did not have to deal with fear, stress, uncertainty, risk, or discomfort to get it?

Think about these questions for every area of your life: home life, work life, social life, financial life, and sex life. In each area, try to visualize your ideal future. Use all of your senses as you visualize. See, hear, feel, and taste it. Get clear about what you want. Then move on to Exercise #2.

BE FEARLESS: *Visualization is a powerful tool. If you see it in your mind, then it's a reality for your body.*

Exercise #2: Write Your Dream List

You just saw your dream, and if you are like most people, what you just saw might scare you a little. It might seem impossible. People often think of reasons why they can't do something rather than why they can. You might find yourself doing the same. The words *can't, shouldn't,* and *won't* might be strong and loud in your head right now. You might be tempted to tell yourself, *I don't really want that. It's a mistake. I don't deserve this.*

Not so fast. That's your fear talking. Remember, now isn't the time to evaluate what you saw.

But it is the time to write it down. If you are fearful of something, writing it down will help you move forward. It takes it out of that hazy place in your mind—that place where denial tends to set in—and moves you a small and painless step closer to action. Writing it down also helps you to organize your thoughts and fine-tune the dream—making it more specific, realistic, and aligned with what you really want. Finally, it helps you stay accountable and committed to the cause.

Sure, writing it down might bring up fear. You might find yourself resisting this exercise. Perhaps you'll say to yourself, *I don't have to write it down; I'll remember it,* or *It's silly to write it down.* It's not silly though.

I write things down, and I find it powerful and effective. I've also watched as client after client grew in courage just by taking the time to write their goals. If you try to keep your dreams and goals in your head, then you can easily procrastinate and ignore them. You can let another day go by before you do anything about them—and then another day and another day, and then eventually a month and then a year. Eventually you'll get to the end of your life and you'll wonder whether or not you have ever really been alive. Having an attitude of "Why do something today that you can put off until tomorrow?" will not make you a success at all. It will only perpetuate you feeling stuck, unhappy, and unfulfilled.

By writing it down, you become more accountable to yourself. Everything becomes more concrete. You start to shift from wishing to doing.

To write your Dream List, take what you learned from Exercise

#1, pick up a pen and your Fearless Notebook, and commit it all to paper. Your list might look like this:

My Dreams
Career:
I want a career that is fulfilling and stimulating.
I want to feel motivated when I get up in the morning. I want to look forward to starting my day at the office.
I want to be in a job where my opinion matters.
Love, Marriage, Relationships:
I want a partner who understands me.
I want to be with someone I can have fun with.
When issues come up, I want to be able to resolve them.
Social Life:
I want to be surrounded by cool friends who get me and support me.
Money:
I want to have enough savings so I can comfortably take vacations.
I want to feel confident about being able to retire.
Sex:
I want to have multiorgasmic earth-shattering sex.
I want to feel so comfortable with my body that I will want to have the lights on.
I want to know that I rock my partner's world.

Make sure you write down everything, even the dreams that you think might be silly, frivolous, impossible, or too scary.

Fear Antidote: Are you drawing a blank? If so, your fear is getting in your way. It's almost as if it's standing behind you, looking over your shoulder, and breathing hot, uncomfortable air down your neck. Who can think freely when that is going on? I know I can't! Here's what to do: dissociate from yourself for a moment. Close your eyes and pretend you are in a movie theater. You are sitting in the back. The room is dark. You are watching the movie on the screen. The main character in the movie is someone a lot like you. This person looks like you. This person has the same personality as you. This person wants the same things in life as you do. And this person is getting them. In this movie, this character has the ideal life. What is it that this person is doing? What are you seeing?

Exercise #3: Strengthen Your Dream List

Until now, I've asked you to turn off that inner critic—that voice in your head that tells you why you can't, shouldn't, or won't do something. I wanted you to do so because, if you allow your critic to surface too early in the process, you'll never get started.

But now you have some momentum. You've written down a number of goals.

It's time to get realistic and figure out which ones are actually goals you can, should, and want to pursue. It's time to let your inner critic have his or her say. Still, I'm going to set some ground rules so your critic doesn't do what he or she normally does and talk you out of every single dream and goal you have. Rather than allow your critic to trash every idea, we're going to guide your critic toward fine-tuning and improving your Dream List.

To do so, we're going to walk through each item on your Dream List one at a time. For each item, think about the following questions, then make any needed changes to your list as a result.

Is this really my dream? Or is it someone else's dream? Think about why you want to pursue this goal. Is it a desire that comes from deep inside? Or is it a desire that comes from outside of yourself—perhaps a desire to please others in your life?

Internally driven motives are far more powerful and lasting than externally driven ones. You'll be a lot more likely to succeed at losing weight, for instance, if you do it because you want to feel more comfortable in your own skin than if you do it to make your spouse fall back in love with you. You'll be a lot more likely to aim for and get a new job if you want the job so you have more autonomy than if you really want the job to impress your friends or family.

Make sure you're setting the goal for yourself and not for someone else or to fulfill societal expectations. Think about whether you listed each goal for the right reasons. Next to each goal, complete this sentence:

I want to do this because _____.

Is your answer about you? Then this is probably an internally motivated goal. Is your answer about someone else? For instance, is this goal about impressing your family or friends? Is it about making you more appealing to a potential mate or more admired? Then it's probably externally motivated, and you will have a much tougher time overcoming your fear and resistance to accomplish this goal. Go through your list and cross off dreams that you might have listed for the wrong reasons. For instance, cross off items that sound like this:

> *I want to become a parent because I want my parents to have a grandchild.*

I want to go to graduate school because that's what everyone else in my family has done, and I don't want to be the family black sheep.

I want to be a stay-at-home mom because I know this would make my husband and my mother very happy.

Is this the right dream? Is there an alternative dream? For each item on the list, think about why you want it and whether there's an alternative way to get what you want. For instance, if you listed "get a new job," think about why. Is it because you hate your current job? If so, is "get a new job" the only possible solution? What about making changes in your current job that might bring you more career satisfaction?

Go through your list. Think about alternatives that could get you to the same goal. Then decide which alternative you feel more inspired to tackle.

Is this dream realistic? You don't want to pick a wildly unrealistic dream. At the same time, you don't want to cave in to your fear of change and decide not to pursue a perfectly attainable dream because your fear tells you, *This is impossible.*

How do you tell the difference? Here are two easy tests.

First, unrealistic dreams tend to be empty. Rather than being tied to your everyday life, they are ideals. For instance, "to become super-rich" is an unrealistic dream for many people. It's also empty because it has little to no meaning. Usually, when people tell me they want to be rich, I find that they really just want to be able to pay their bills without worrying about going into debt and be comfortable enough to splurge on something every now and then. What they really want isn't necessarily wealth. It's financial security, and financial security is a lot easier to attain than becoming super-rich.

Second, unrealistic dreams usually require huge leaps forward, whereas attainable ones can easily be broken down into small, doable minigoals, which I like to call stepping-stones. For each item on your list, think about whether you can come up with at least three small actions you can take toward your dream. For instance, let's say one of the items on your list is "write a book." Three small actions toward writing a book might be: (1) decide what I want to write about; (2) read books on writing a book; and (3) write about my topic for fifteen minutes every day. All three of those steps seem perfectly doable and reasonable to me. I'm guessing they do to you as well.

On the other hand, let's say your dream is to date and marry Brad Pitt. (I know this is an extreme example.) Can you come up with three small strategies you can do relatively simply and easily to get yourself closer to achieving that goal? Unless your name happens to be Angelina Jolie, I doubt you can.

> **BE FEARLESS:** *As the ancient Chinese philosopher Lao-tzu once said, "A journey of a thousand miles begins with one step." If you can come up with a few small steps, then you can probably come up with a thousand more.*

If you can't come up with a single small step, chances are that you will not be able to get to your destination. Think long and hard about each item on your list. Is it possible? If so, why? Is it impossible? If so, why?

Is this dream inspiring? Did it come from a place of inspiration or a place of desperation? You are doing them out of inspiration if your dreams are about moving toward something positive, whereas you are doing them out of desperation if your dreams are about moving away from something negative.

Inspiring dreams sound like this:

*I want to become a writer because I've always loved words.
I love them so much that I've been writing as a hobby for
years.*

*I would love to own my own home. I would love the sense of
autonomy that it would give me.*

*I would be thrilled if I could travel the world. I have always
loved learning about other cultures and exploring other
countries. I really want to bring travel back into my life.*

On the other hand, you are coming from a place of desperation
if your goals sound like this:

I should get married because I am scared of being alone.

*I'd better get a promotion at work because I don't know what
will happen if I don't.*

*If I don't move across the country, I might end up feeling
miserable for the rest of my life.*

You may think that desperation and inspiration are equally
motivating, but they are not. Desperation is a short-term motivator
at best. It's rarely strong enough to help anyone fully disengage
from fear. When most people use desperation to motivate themselves, they end up forming an on-again, off-again relationship
with fear. They start to make a change. Then they regress. Then
they try again. Then they backslide.

On the other hand, people who use inspiration as their main
motivator remain positive and think long-term. They are able to
overcome short-term discomfort and anxiety because they know
the long-term goal is so worth it.

To figure out if your dreams and goals are inspiring, take a
look at your Dream List and notice whether you've used inspiring
words or desperate words to describe your dreams.

Inspiring Words and Phrases	Desperate Words and Phrases
It will be great when...	I have to...
I'm looking forward to...	I should...
I can't wait until...	If I don't do it then...
I'm so psyched that I get to...	I'd better, or else...

Is this a positive dream or goal? It's more motivating to focus on what you will do with your life than it is to focus on what you won't do or will stop doing. In fact, the more you focus on not doing something, the more you will want to do it. Think of the magical attraction of a "confidential" label on an envelope and you'll know precisely what I mean. Or think of how you feel when someone says, "I'd love to tell you about this, but it's a secret. Let's forget I ever brought it up."

Um, forget? Really? Now you can't stop thinking about it! Right?

This is why I want you to take a look at each goal on your list and rewrite it to make it positive. Here are some examples for you to use as inspiration.

Negative Goal	Positive Goal
I won't put myself out as much.	I will prioritize and find balance.
I won't be a doormat at work.	I will assert myself.
I won't get anxious on dates.	I will be relaxed and comfortable on dates.
I won't get behind on bills.	I will organize my finances.
I won't eat chocolate and potato chips.	I will eat healthy foods such as fruit and nuts.

Is this goal specific? The more specific your goal, the more likely you will stick with it. Vague goals such as "I want to be happier" provide nothing precise to commit to. It's far better to spell it out and define what you mean by *happier*. What does *happier* mean to you? Does it mean that you have autonomy at work and financial freedom? That you will be in control of your schedule? That you will have time for yourself once a day every day? That you will feel grateful for what's good in your life? Or that you will think positive thoughts more than half of the time? Really spell it out. Get as precise as you can.

Take yet another look at your Dream List. Go through each item again. This time make your goals and dreams as specific as possible. To make them more specific, think about the following questions:

- What does this dream look like?
- What does it feel like to achieve this dream?
- How will it change my life?
- What will I be doing differently when I have this dream come true for me?

Make each item on your list as specific as possible. Use the following chart for ideas on how to go from vague to specific.

Vague Goal	How to Get Specific	Specific Goal
I want a better job	Define *better*	I want a job that pays $10,000 more a year, allows me to be creative, and gives me more responsibility and autonomy.

Vague Goal	How to Get Specific	Specific Goal
Meet a great guy	Define *great guy*	I want to meet a guy who is a good listener, is supportive, and shares similar interests.
Get in shape	Define *in shape*	I want to be able to walk without getting winded, be able to touch my toes, and pick up my kids without throwing out my back.

Put Your Dream to the Test

Place a check mark next to each dream on your list that has the following characteristics. The more checkmarks you have next to a dream, the more likely you will turn that dream into a reality.

✓ **Internally motivated.** That means you are reaching for this dream because you want it and not because someone else wants it for you.

✓ **Appropriate.** This goal is the best way to get where you want to go. There are no more appropriate alternatives.

✓ **Realistic.** You can think of at least one small action you can take right now that will get you a little closer to this goal.

✓ **Inspiring.** This goal inspires you to change. You are excited about moving toward something rather than desperate to move away from it.

continued

✓ **Positive.** It's about something you will do rather than something you want to stop doing.

✓ **Specific.** You've defined this dream. You know what it looks, feels, and sounds like. It is crystal clear.

Exercise #4: Fear-proof Your Dream List

Now you've got all of these goals committed to paper. Chances are you are feeling a little anxious because you are starting to sense what is coming soon: change.

Change is scary. That's why I want you to fear-proof your Dream List. This exercise involves thinking of the payoff for tackling each goal on your list. By doing so, you'll be able to continually look beyond your fear of the short term. The process is very similar to what many athletes do when they are attempting to motivate themselves to keep going despite overwhelming fatigue and discomfort. Rather than focus on everything they are experiencing in the now, they look forward to the future—and to their ultimate goal.

To better understand the power of this, take a moment to think about what you might do if you were running a marathon and you were at mile 20. Imagine that your feet hurt. You're hot. You're tired. You're uncomfortable, and you really want to quit.

How do you think you might motivate yourself to keep going? What do you think you would do?

Did you come up with any of the following?

- Think about the celebratory beer, ice cream, or pizza you are going to eat once you cross the finish line.
- Think about the sense of accomplishment you will feel when you put that finisher's medal around your neck.

- Think of how proud you will feel when you are able to tell your friends and family that you made it.

Rather than continually focus on how crappy you feel and on the short-term stress and discomfort, you would focus on all of the gains and benefits that lie ahead, wouldn't you? You'd continually remind yourself of the long-term gain.

And that's precisely what I want you to do now. Until now you've been mired in the short term. You've only seen and responded to the short-term dangers, stress, and discomfort. It's time to move beyond all of that and motivate yourself toward your own finish line.

BE FEARLESS: *It's better to deal with short-term stress than it is to deal with long-term misery.*

This exercise will help you to do just that. By writing down all of the benefits of changing, you will be able to motivate yourself to keep moving forward. When you think, *What if she rejects me?* you'll be able to look at your Payoff List and say, "No matter how much that stings, it will be worth it because I know I gave it my best and won't have any regrets."

Find a fresh sheet of paper in your Fearless Notebook. Jot down all of your dreams again, using a two-column format. In the first column list the dream. In the second, write down all of the payoffs of reaching that dream. To come up with payoffs, imagine what your life will be like once you make that dream a reality. How will your life change? How will it be different? What's the benefit of achieving this dream for you? How will your life be once you complete this task? What will you gain from it? How will your day-to-day life change? How will your relationships change with colleagues, with siblings, or with your partner? How will the sixteen hours that you are awake every day be different?

When coming up with payoffs, keep the following in mind:

Keep them positive. You'll be motivated more by long-term positive gains than you will by avoiding short-term negative problems. In other words, "I'll have the chance to meet new and interesting people" is more motivating than "I won't have to put up with this crap anymore."

Focus on the long term. It's the short term that will be uncomfortable. You want payoffs that you can see one month, six months, and one year or more from now.

If you have trouble coming up with payoffs, think about this question: *How would my life be if fear were not a factor?*

Use this Payoff List as an example for inspiration in coming up with your own.

Dream	Payoffs
Overcome my fear of going to medical school	I will prove to myself that I can become anything and end up with a fulfilling career that allows me to make a difference.
Run a marathon	I'll get in shape, gain a sense of accomplishment, and be able to say to myself, *If I did this, I can do anything.*
Become self-employed	I'll be my own boss, make my own hours, and make all of the decisions. I can wear what I want, won't have to deal with performance reviews, and will have a sense of pride in what I do for a living.

Dream	Payoffs
Overcome my fear of flying	I'll be able to see the world and go to places I've only read about. I'll also be able to visit relatives I haven't seen in a long time. I'll even be able to move up at work because I'll be able to travel and take on more responsibility.

Exercise #5: Prioritize Your Dream List

Now it's time to figure out which dream you are going to tackle first. To do so, assign each item on your list a number ranging from one to five.

1 = I really can't find a way to live without it. I must achieve this dream as soon as possible.

2 = This dream excites me, and I'd love to see it happen at some point in the next six months.

3 = This dream would be so cool, but other dreams on my list would be even cooler.

4 = I really want to do this, but I don't mind waiting to make it happen.

5 = I'd love to have this, sure, but I could still be happy without it.

Note: Be careful about assigning lots of fives. Your fearful mind might nudge you into thinking that you can wait to achieve everything on your list because it fears what might happen if you tackle one of those items today.

Fear Antidote: Think of the most courageous person you know.

Then whenever you find your fear talking you out of turning a page or doing an exercise, imagine that you are this person. What would this courageous person do right now? Would this person give up? Put the book down? Skip an exercise because it brought up too much emotional resistance? Or would this person become complacent and accept the status quo? I'm guessing that this person would keep moving forward. How about you?

How Do You Feel?

You did it! You just completed Step 1 of the program. I hope you are feeling good about yourself. What you just did was very challenging. You had to overcome some fear in order to see and define your dreams. That's huge. So give yourself a pat on the back and feel good.

Also remember this accomplishment. I hope that it will serve as the first of many pieces of evidence for you that you really can face your fear. You can end this codependent relationship and persevere through short-term discomfort. You have it in you. You just proved it to yourself by completing this first step.

Let's keep the momentum going. Now it's time to get started on Step 2.

Fearless Makeover

Anne, in her forties, was an educated and talented advertising sales professional who worked in a male-dominated business. Her company was male-run, and she had done quite well, but could do much better.

The Goal: Anne wanted to advance in her career and overcome what was holding her back.

The Payoff: If Anne overcame what was holding her back, she would make more money, get promoted to a position she wanted, and feel more in control of her career.

The Program: Anne worried that becoming too successful would lead to loneliness. "If I'm hugely successful and powerful, then people won't like me. They'll attack me, question me, or be jealous," she said. Anne was uncertain about her future, and this uncertainty scared her. She had a fear of the unknown, and she made false assumptions that magnified, perpetuated, and supported her fear.

I asked Anne to define success (Step 1). I asked, "What does it mean to you?" She answered, "It means making a lot of money. Reaching the top of my game and full potential." I then asked her to write a list of people who she felt would be supportive of her success along with another list of people who might be jealous. She listed her family and friends on the supportive side, but men on the nonsupportive side. She felt that men would be jealous of her success.

I knew these were just excuses and not reality. Anne's fear of success wasn't truly about men. It was about an underlying fear of recognition. She told me, "People might think I'm a fraud. How will I sustain my success? Do I even deserve this?"

This type of thinking is common. Frequently people attribute their success to circumstances and to others rather than to their hard work and talent. Anne was no exception. I told her that her fear of success led to procrastination, and this had become a cycle for her. Her procrastination led to avoidance of

continued

the anxiety-provoking fear, which was more comfortable than doing what she needed to do, which was face it.

"Tell me about a recent success that you had at work," I said.

She replied, "My sales numbers were the highest for the last quarter."

I asked, "What did you do to get there?"

She told me the specifics. I then asked, "Who helped you get there?" knowing full well that she'd done it on her own.

She proudly said, "I did it by myself."

I asked her to make a list of all of the skills and talents that she used to make this success possible (Step 2).

She did. She realized that she wasn't a fraud. She really did have skills and talents that led to her being successful.

The Outcome: Anne continued to overcome her fear of success and later was promoted to regional vice president of her company. She eventually found love too. As I'd expected, there really were men out there who were not jealous of or threatened by successful women.

Chapter Seven

Step 2: Break Your Fear Pattern

If you are like many people, then you've gotten roughly this far several times before. You identified the dream. You wrote it down. Heck you might have even gone through magazines, clipped photos and headlines, taped it all together, and created one of those vision boards that were all the rage not too long ago.

There was no question about where you wanted to go, but you just didn't get there. You weren't able to move forward.

You probably blamed yourself for this failure. Perhaps you told yourself that you just didn't want it badly enough, that you lack motivation and willpower, or that you aren't cut out for change. But that's nonsense. I'm quite certain that you wanted your dreams to come true just as much as anyone else. I'm also pretty sure that you gave it your all. You didn't hold back. You were motivated and you had plenty of willpower. You went for it.

But you didn't succeed because you didn't know how to shift from thinking to doing. You didn't know how to create a strategy— one that would help you get results. Because of this, you relied on what you knew, what others recommended, and even what plenty of self-help books promote: wishful thinking. As I've mentioned, this type of thinking keeps you stuck because it assigns the control of your life over to an amorphous, invisible, unpredictable entity.

You don't reach goals by wishing for them, and you don't overcome fear by wishing for it to go away either. You make dreams come true by creating a strategic plan and following it until you achieve results. Steps 2 through 5 will help you create and execute that plan.

Step 2 in particular will help you to face your fear of change. Change of any kind is scary, stressful, and requires work and effort. You are going to feel anxious and get freaked out when you confront your fear and try to move forward. But Step 2 will take a lot of the fearful bite out of change. This step is going to help you to weaken the hold that fear has had on you until now. It will help you to motivate yourself in the direction you want to go—no matter how much stress, anxiety, or discomfort you might experience along the way.

Of course I'd be lying if I promised you that confronting your fear would be a cakewalk. If you want a cakewalk, then keep using wishful thinking. If you actually want to overcome your fear, reach your goals, and make your dreams come true, then keep reading.

Change Your Life in Less Than Two Hours!

Step 2 includes four exercises that will take you anywhere from one to two hours to complete. I encourage you to block off a chunk of time for these exercises and do them one after the other. They all relate to one another. Check them off as you move forward.

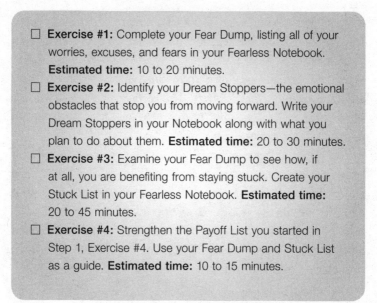

☐ **Exercise #1:** Complete your Fear Dump, listing all of your worries, excuses, and fears in your Fearless Notebook. **Estimated time:** 10 to 20 minutes.

☐ **Exercise #2:** Identify your Dream Stoppers—the emotional obstacles that stop you from moving forward. Write your Dream Stoppers in your Notebook along with what you plan to do about them. **Estimated time:** 20 to 30 minutes.

☐ **Exercise #3:** Examine your Fear Dump to see how, if at all, you are benefiting from staying stuck. Create your Stuck List in your Fearless Notebook. **Estimated time:** 20 to 45 minutes.

☐ **Exercise #4:** Strengthen the Payoff List you started in Step 1, Exercise #4. Use your Fear Dump and Stuck List as a guide. **Estimated time:** 10 to 15 minutes.

Exercise #1: Do a Fear Dump

In this initial exercise, I'm going to ask you to do something that is quite counterintuitive. Many therapists would even tell you that this is ridiculous and bad for you. But I've seen this exercise transform client after client. That's how I know it will work for you.

The exercise is counterintuitive because it involves feeding your fear. Bear with me.

Take a look at the Dream List you created in Step 1. Then, on a fresh piece of paper in your Fearless Notebook, do a Fear Dump for each of your prioritized dreams. Write down all of the reasons you think you can't or won't be able to make this dream a reality in your life.

Seriously, let it rip. List every single nagging concern. Give me every single excuse you've got. Talk me out of forcing you to go for it. Argue with me. Plead. Get it all out there. Purge every single fearful thought, anxious reaction, doubt, and bit of negativity from your system.

Are you already arguing with me in your mind? Maybe you're saying, *Jonathan, this is crazy. You've been talking about the importance of thinking positive and here you are suggesting I go negative? I can't do this!*

Yes, you can. Sure, eventually I want you to get to a positive place. But you can't get to positive without first acknowledging and understanding the negative. If you try to ignore the negative and pretend like it's not there, any positive thinking you do will be about as effective as a surgeon putting a Band-Aid on a severed limb. The flow of negativity will overwhelm your efforts to think positive and eventually wear you down.

So don't hold back. Write down every single negative, self-defeating thought. Write down every fear, every bit of mental resistance, and every excuse. Look at your Dream List and ask, "Why can't I do this? What will stop me from doing this? Why shouldn't I do this? Why won't I do this?"

For help and inspiration, let's take a look at how three of my clients created their Fear Dumps.

Let's start with Lori, a thirty-eight-year-old married mother of two kids, ages eight and five. She worked in retail because it always fit best with her husband's work schedule and allowed her to be there for her kids. When I asked her about her job, her response was like a broken record. She just kept saying, "It works." When I asked her what she would want to do if she wasn't just doing what works, she replied with great enthusiasm, "I always wanted to be a teacher!" She had a passion for art and kids, and she wanted to be an art teacher. I suggested she might pursue this as a dream, and I helped her overcome the fear associated with switching careers.

What follows is Lori's Fear Dump. From it, you can easily see just how much energy Lori was putting into maintaining a life that wasn't working for her. Once she finally dumped all of this negativity, she was able to see that this dream really was something she wanted to pursue.

Lori's Fear Dump

I can't afford to go to school. We won't be able to pay the bills.
I don't have enough time to do this. I should wait until the kids are older.
I'm too old to go back to school.
I don't deserve this. I decided to be a housewife and I need to stick to the plan.
I'm selfish for wanting this. I should just be content with my life the way it is.
I'm not strong enough to go after this.
I was such a poor student. What makes me think I can be a teacher?

Now, let's take a look at Jake. Jake wanted to get out of a dead-end relationship with his longtime girlfriend. He knew she wasn't right for him, and he wanted to end the relationship so he could be free to find someone who might be a better fit. Still, fear held him back. He'd broken up with his girlfriend a few times in the past only to go back to her. He told me that he'd wanted to break up with her for good for the past six months, but he just couldn't bring himself to do it.

This is what he wrote in his Fear Dump:

Jake's Fear Dump

We have fun together.
We know each other so well. Do I really want to give that up?
I've invested a lot of time in this relationship.
I've invested a lot of energy into this relationship.

*The sex is great. The best I've ever had. If we break up, I might
   not get any sex for a while.*

*What if I can't find someone new? Maybe I can't find anyone
   better.*

What if I end up being alone for the rest of my life?

*The thought of going out there and meeting new people fright-
   ens me.*

I don't even know how to break up.

She'll be mad at me.

I don't want to hurt her.

Finally let's take a look at one more Fear Dump. This one comes
from Stacy. She was thirty-two years old when I began counseling her, and she told me she'd always wanted to run a marathon.
Still, fear held her back. In high school she ran cross-country and
track. She'd also completed a few 10K races in college and during
her late twenties. But she'd been talking about this marathon for
years and could not seem to commit to it. She kept vaguely telling friends that she was going to sign up for the New York City
Marathon. Then the registration deadline would pass without her
sending hers in. This is what she wrote in her Fear Dump:

Stacy's Fear Dump

I'm so out of shape.

I'm too old for this.

My friends will think I'm crazy.

I don't have time to train.

I have no idea how to even train for a marathon.

My relationship will suffer.

*No one I know has ever run a marathon. Why the heck do I
   think I can do it?*

It will take me all day to complete it!

Use Stacy's, Lori's, and Jake's Fear Dumps to help you construct your own. Remember: don't hold back. Put it all out there. This should feel good. Get this fear out of your system!

Exercise #2: Overcome Your Dream Stoppers

Your Fear Dump is important because it's going to help you to identify your Dream Stoppers. Dream Stoppers are emotional obstacles that prevent you from moving forward. They are like stop signs for the mind, but placed there unnecessarily. Your Dream Stoppers are ingrained, habitual, and automatic. You've been defaulting to and relying on these Stoppers for years. You probably don't even know you are using them.

Think of your Dream Stoppers like a light switch that doesn't work when the power is out. How many times have you flipped the light switch even though you know they aren't going to work? You probably keep reaching for it and flipping it into the on position. You don't do this because you think flipping the switch is actually going to get you your desired result. No, you do it because it's automated. You do it without thinking.

Dream Stoppers are the same. You are so used to them that you might not even be aware that you are using them or that they are keeping you mired and stuck. That's why this exercise will be so freeing and powerful for you. It's going to help you identify and weaken your Dream Stoppers so you can finally overcome them and move forward.

In counseling many fearful clients over the years, I've been able to document six common Stoppers. If you are stuck, you are defaulting to one or more of these Stoppers on a regular basis. And while the Dream Stoppers are all a little different from one another, they share a common trait: negativity. Remember the negativity bias I mentioned earlier. Dream Stoppers cause you to see the dangers associated with facing your fear. Your Dream Stoppers fill your mind with *I can't because...* When you spend too much time focusing on the negatives and all of the reasons why you *can't* do something, you feed your fear and you starve your motivation. You end up talking yourself into staying stuck and out of moving forward.

Your Dream Stoppers prevent you from seeing the huge benefits of facing your fear. Yes, there really are huge benefits for facing your fears, and you'll learn about them soon.

Once you understand your Dream Stoppers, you'll be better able to interrupt and override them. You'll weaken and break them so they lose their power over you. Rather than fixating on why you can't, won't, or shouldn't do something, you'll be able to continually and strongly remind yourself of why you can, will, and should pursue your dreams.

> **BE FEARLESS:** *Focus on why you can, should, and will accomplish your dream, and not on why you can't, shouldn't, or won't.*

And in doing so you'll experience a lot less stress, anxiety, and resistance.

I'd like you to read about the following six Dream Stoppers. As you learn about each Stopper, take a look at your Fear Dump. Based on your Fear Dump, you'll be able to identify which Stoppers are preventing you from moving forward.

Stopper #1: You See Yourself Living Unhappily Ever After

This is your Stopper if your mind fixates on tragedy and peril whenever you think about pursuing your dream. You have the mind of a true crime novelist, one who continually writes plots that star you as the victim.

As you've learned, our brains don't like uncertainty. As a result, the brain does whatever it can do to create certainty and predictability. When you are stuck in the Unhappily Ever After Stopper, your brain is attempting to create certainty and predictability by falsely predicting outcomes. Problem is, they are always negative.

For instance, let's say you go on a date and you think it went very well. Then you don't hear back from the guy for a few days. If you then have the following thoughts, your brain is definitely defaulting to the Unhappily Ever After Stopper: "He's just not into me" or "He must be married" or "He must be gay." These explanations help to eliminate the uncertainty by providing what seems like a plausible explanation. And while these explanations might be plausible, they are no more likely than a more positive explanation. It's just as likely that he's not married or gay and that he really is into you, isn't it? Couldn't it be just as possible that he's just been busy, out of town, dealing with an emergency, or even just worried about coming on too strong?

You might have this Stopper if: Your Fear Dump is riddled with negative predictions. For instance, in Jake's Fear Dump, you can see the Unhappily Ever After Stopper when he writes, "What if I end up alone for the rest of my life?" and "She'll be mad at me." In Stacy's, you can see it in her comment "My relationship will suffer." In Lori's, you can see this Stopper in her comment, "We won't be able to pay the bills."

Why it stops you: The Unhappily Ever After Stopper creates fear while killing confidence. Negative predictions are quite de-motivating. By scripting your Unhappily Ever After before it actually happens, you encourage yourself to give up, a move that eventually leads to the undesirable result that you most fear.

How to break the pattern: Next time you find yourself using this Stopper, ask yourself, *Where's the evidence to support this belief? Is there evidence to the contrary? What are alternative, more positive explanations? Is there a way for me to write a Happily Ever After for myself rather than an Unhappily Ever After?* For instance, with Lori's "I won't be able to pay the bills" prediction, it's just as likely that, "I'll find a way to do this by budgeting my money and cutting costs."

Stopper #2: You Give Yourself a Failing Grade

Do your excuses from your Fear Dump center on a personal flaw you see in yourself? For instance, is your Fear Dump filled with blaming statements like "I'm not good enough" and "I don't deserve this"?

If so, then you might be overpersonalizing. When you default to the Failing Grade Stopper, you are too quick to blame yourself and jump to a conclusion that you are the reason something did or didn't happen. For instance, a friend of mine used to teach piano. She had a student who just wasn't learning. Week after week it was the same. The student would show up and be just as bad at playing the same material. It didn't seem to matter what she told him or what she suggested. This student just didn't improve.

My friend began to lose confidence. "I'm a bad teacher," she told me. "I don't even know what I'm doing wrong. That's how bad I am." Her issues with this one student began eroding her self-confidence. Soon she was nervous before every single lesson, and the nervousness showed. This became a vicious cycle and soon she was fearful of giving lessons.

She was fearful of doing something that she was actually quite good at.

In reality, she was never the problem. The student was not interested in learning piano and only showed up each week because his parents forced him to take the lessons. He didn't pay attention to what my friend taught him, and he didn't practice at home either. So he never improved. Yet my friend blamed herself, and this eroded her confidence. This is the epitome of personalization.

You might have this Stopper if: From your Fear Dump, you see lots of statements that blame you as the problem. Your excuses will lead you to believe you are the reason this dream is not possible. You'll see phrases like "I can't do this" and "I'm not good at _____" and "Because of me this can't happen." For instance, in Lori's Fear Dump, you can see the Failing Grade Stopper in her excuse, "I was such a poor student. What makes me think I can be a teacher?"

Why it stops you: This personalization can render you fearful and hesitant to try new things. You are allowing yourself only a narrow view by blaming yourself. This narrow view doesn't allow you to explore other reasons that are less damaging to your self-esteem and confidence. By maintaining this negative view, you demotivate yourself and stop yourself from trying harder or moving forward.

How to break the pattern: The remedy here is similar to the remedy for Stopper #1. Break yourself out of seeing things only one way. Ask yourself, *What are other possible explanations? Could there be another reason for this? Is it possible that I am really capable of more than I give myself credit for?* Think of all of the reasons that have nothing to do with you.

Here's something else you can try. For every failing grade you've given yourself, think back over your life and look for evidence to the contrary. For instance, if you've written, "I'm not strong enough to...," then think back over your life and come up with times when you were stronger than you thought you could be. Or if the statement says, "I can't...," think about a time in your life when you thought you couldn't do something and then you did it anyway. For instance, maybe you couldn't ride a bike on your first try, but you eventually mastered it. Maybe you couldn't learn a new language at first, but you eventually got it down.

Think back over your life and think about everything you've faced, learned, and accomplished that you initially didn't think you could do. List as many examples as you can in your Fearless Notebook. Keep this list handy because you might need to refer to it over and over again to remind yourself that you are stronger, smarter, and more persistent than you believe.

You can also use the following advice:

- **Test your belief that you don't deserve your success.** Ask yourself, *How did I get to where I am? Who helped me?* If you did this on your own, the evidence suggests that you do deserve to be where you are.
- **Focus on your strengths.** List your skills, strengths, and talents that you've used so far to make your current level of success possible.
- **Normalize your thinking.** It's okay to feel in over your head. This is how many people feel whenever they start something new. You are not the only one. More important, the feeling is temporary. Once you get used to your new responsibilities, it will pass.
- **Shift your thinking.** Don't think, *What will I do if they find out I'm incompetent?* Do think, *I might not be 100 percent on top of my game right now, but I am going to give it my best. It's normal to feel slightly off at first.*

Stopper #3: You Always Color Inside the Lines

If I had to teach a mother how to instill fear in her child, I would tell her to give the child a set of absolute rules—rules that must be followed all the time, no matter the circumstances. You may have even encountered children who have been given such rules. If so, then you know what I mean. They are timid and anxious. They are constantly worried about doing the wrong thing and getting in trouble. They are attempting to follow rules that they don't understand and didn't make. Because they don't understand these rules, they are filled with anxiety and will start sobbing when they break one—for instance, by coloring outside the lines.

Children are not the only people who have the Color Inside the Lines Stopper, though. Plenty of adults have it also. When you suffer from this Stopper, you see life as a series of rules or commandments—rules that must be followed 100 percent of the time. Either you follow them exactly or your life will fall apart. When I hear statements such as "I need to ...," "I should ...," or "I could never ...," then I know I'm dealing with someone who only colors inside the lines. This is a person with high standards, rigid thinking, and expectations that are unreasonable or unrealistic.

> **BE FEARLESS:** *There's no such thing as perfect—it's just a perpetual quest to find what's wrong with something.*

Anything that deviates from these rules will produce anxiety. As soon as you start thinking about possibilities—possibilities that fall outside of the bounds—you feel fear and anxiety and find yourself asking questions like, *How can I do that? How could I ever face that?*

You might have this Stopper if: From you Fear Dump, you notice a lot of sentences that start with the words *need to, should,* and *I could never*. For instance, in Lori's Fear Dump, you can see this Dream Stopper when she writes, "I should wait until the kids are older," "I decided to be a housewife and I need to stick to the plan," and "I should just be content with my life the way it is."

Why it stops you: If you hold out for perfect, you will be waiting forever. The only person who thinks you should or should not do something is you. It's really okay to change the rules and to color outside the lines. Doing so provides more options.

How to break the pattern: For every commandment or rule on your Fear Dump, I want you to write down a new rule that counters it. For instance, in Lori's Fear Dump, her rule "I should wait until the kids are older," could be countered with this: "But if I do it now, I'll be in a better position to be involved with the kids when they are teens. If I am a teacher, I will have the same schedule that they will have, so I will be able to keep an eye on them."

Stopper #4: You Have Compliment Amnesia

I counsel many accomplished people who seemingly have everything to feel good about. They are at the top of their careers. They are good-looking. They are surrounded by adoring family and friends. People often tell them, "I think you are awesome."

Yet these folks don't feel awesome. When they come to my office they tell me that they are losers and failures and that no one likes them. They are filled with fear because they've developed a negative view of themselves. They are not able to grow or progress. They are always discounting success and compliments, and they stay stuck as a result.

I often ask people with Compliment Amnesia, "Has anyone ever told you you are good at what you do?" They downplay or reject these compliments, saying things such as "They're just being nice" or "They just say these things because they feel sorry for me."

Then I follow up with, "How does your cousin describe you? How does your mother describe you? How do your friends describe you? How do your coworkers describe you?"

Often the evidence will start to mount, showing that they really are deserving of these compliments after all.

"Do these people have any reason to lie? Do they have reasons to tell the truth?" I ask. "If several people are saying the same thing and they all have reasons to tell you the truth, maybe this really is the truth."

You might have this Stopper if: You cling to the word *but*. For instance, you might think, "People tell me I'm smart, *but* that's really not true." Or someone compliments you, and you say, "Yeah, but . . ."

Why it stops you: It prevents you from enjoying the moment and feeling good about yourself. When you don't feel good about yourself, you are less likely to pursue your goals and dreams.

How to break the pattern: Try this next time you find yourself suffering from Compliment Amnesia. Make a list of your strengths and the things that you're good at. Keep these things in mind. They're all you. Own them! Also whenever you find yourself using the word *but*, eliminate that word and everything that comes after it. For instance, instead of saying, "People tell me that I'm brilliant, *but* they are just saying that to make me feel good," stop just before the *but* and say, "People tell me I'm brilliant." Period.

Stopper #5: You Think in Two Shades: Black and White

When I was a kid, my family used to go to a bakery and we'd pick up black-and-white cookies. These were cookies where half of the cookie top was glazed with chocolate and the other with vanilla. They're still around today. You might wonder what the heck a cookie has to do with a Stopper. As it turns out, a lot!

I often see people who live as if their lives were black and white cookies. They only ever give themselves two opposing options:

- Right or wrong
- True or false
- Yes or no
- Good or bad
- Fat or thin
- Smart or dumb
- Rich or poor
- Winner or loser
- Success or failure

This not only leads to a dull existence, it also creates fear. Every small problem or complication is perceived as a huge failure because they only give themselves two options—either they are a complete success or a total failure. They don't see the huge gray area in between those two options.

A Black or White Thinker who gets A− on a test thinks, "I'm no good." A Black or White Thinker who comes in second place feels bad, saying something like, "Second is the first loser."

You might have this Stopper if: You are uncomfortable with the middle ground and you quickly discount its existence when someone points it out. If you are not at the top, you find it anxiety provoking. From your Fear Dump, you'll see statements like, "I don't know if I can be the best" and "I'll never be good at this." You will also find that you tend to procrastinate. Your desire to make things perfect or the best will cause you to continually put things off until the moment is "just right." You might find that you also have issues with writer's block, stage fright, and other types of performance anxiety due to your desire to always be the best.

Why it stops you: Life is about the middle. It's very rare for anyone to be on the extreme—either at the complete top or at the complete bottom. If you shoot for perfection, you will nearly always be disappointed and fearful of falling short of your goal. It will be a never-ending quest.

How to break the pattern: Look over your Fear Dump for this type of extreme thinking. See if you can find a middle ground between the two extremes. List as many options that fall between your two extremes as you can think of. Then try a few out. See what happens when you are okay with the middle.

Stopper #6: You Make Decisions Based on a Sample of One

When my beloved grandmother Helen was young, she got a headache after eating chocolate. She never ate another piece of chocolate again. That one incident caused her to link "chocolate" with "headache." It became a bad reference experience for her, one that she carried with her until her death at age ninety-four.

One of my friends told me that when she was a teen she danced to a song during a pool party. Two other adolescents laughed at her and told her she couldn't dance. From that day forward, she felt nervous and self-conscious on the dance floor. For most of her adulthood, she told people, "I don't dance" and "I can't dance." Then, not long ago, she took a Zumba dance class. It was there when she realized that she wasn't such a bad dancer after all. After the class, various women came up to her and made comments about her dancing ability, marveling, "I can't believe this was your first class. You were so good!" And she had refused to dance for all of those years just because of that one incident that had taken place when she was a teenager!

Similarly, I've told you about the time when I was six and the poodle chased me down the street. It's a funny story, especially because of the breed of the dog. But it wasn't funny to me at the time, and it wasn't funny for many years, as that one experience colored my view of dogs in general. I thought they were all as vicious as that mean poodle, and I kept my distance.

These are all examples of negative reference experiences. I've found that of all of the Dream Stoppers, this one is the most common. Most people have suffered from this Dream Stopper in one or more areas of their lives. They draw a conclusion based on a sample size of one.

Let's take a look at how a false conclusion can be reached based on one experience:

I got a headache after eating chocolate = I can't eat chocolate.
Two girls laughed at me = I am a terrible dancer.
A poodle once chased me = All dogs are vicious.

What's sad about these negative reference experiences is that, for most people, they've taken place five, ten, or twenty or more years ago. But these isolated experiences still affect how they live (or don't live) their lives today.

You might have this Stopper if: You are basing a future prediction on a past event, and one event from many years ago is coloring your view of yourself today. From your Fear Dump, you'll be able to see this Stopper in statements like, "But I'm just not good at..." and "But I could never do that..." From Lori's Fear Dump, the statement "I'm not strong enough to go after this" is a sign that she might have this Stopper.

Why it stops you: When you give yourself only one frame of reference, you filter out other possibilities, and you stop yourself from pursuing what you really want and what you are really capable of achieving. You tell yourself that you just "aren't good" at any number of things that you probably could become quite good at if you gave yourself the chance.

How to break the pattern: Look at your Fear Dump and find phrases like "I can't..." and "I'm not ___ enough" and "I could never..." Think back over your life and try to identify the negative reference experience that led to this belief. This might take a little time, but eventually you'll pinpoint it. Once you do, ask yourself, *Was this an isolated event? Am I basing an entire lifetime of choices on a sample size of one?* Good researchers do not conduct studies based on sample sizes of one. You don't want to draw your conclusions based on a sample size of one either. So allow yourself to enlarge the sample size. Have there been other experiences that contradict this view? Also deconstruct the reference experience. Are there reasons for this negative experience that have nothing to do with you? For instance, when my friend deconstructed hers, she realized that the two girls who laughed at her were envious of her and just wanted to take her down a peg. It had nothing to do with her inherent dancing ability.

Write Down Your Stoppers

In your Fearless Notebook, write down which of the following six Stoppers you tend to default to, along with how you plan to break the pattern.

- **The Unhappily Ever After Stopper.** You fixate on tragedy and peril whenever you think about pursuing your dream.
- **The Failing Grade Stopper.** You overpersonalize failure and life problems, seeing everything that goes wrong as a personal failing.
- **The Color Inside the Lines Stopper.** You see life as a series of rules that must be followed 100 percent of the

continued

time. If you break a rule, you experience stress, anxiety, and panic.

- **The Compliment Amnesia Stopper.** No matter what anyone says about you, you know you are no good.
- **The Black-and-White Stopper.** You only ever give yourself two opposing options such as right or wrong and good or bad.
- **The Sample of One Stopper.** You avoid situations and people because of one bad experience.

Exercise #3: Acknowledge Your Codependent Relationship with Fear

You will probably find that your Dream Stoppers are as dear to you as they are dysfunctional. When you think about parting with them, you might experience a sense of emptiness or of being out of control.

That's because many people have a codependent relationship with their fear, and they benefit from using it as an excuse. For instance, a fearful person might avoid going to a party because she's "bad with people" or not apply for a job because "I'm not good with responsibility." But these excuses are rarely, if ever, based on reality. The socially anxious person can be good with people, and the person with a fear of rejection can be good with responsibility, too. They choose to believe these excuses, however, because the excuses allow them to stay stuck and avoid feeling uncomfortable.

When you finally walk away from fear, it will feel as if you are walking away from any dysfunctional relationship. You know that you want to end the relationship. You know that you need to end the relationship. But it's not going to be easy. You're benefiting from this relationship, and you will feel uncomfortable, stressed, and/or anxious when you walk away from those benefits.

It's for this precise reason that so many people have a hard time walking away from what they already know is bad for them. It's why smokers have a hard time quitting. It's why some people stay in abusive relationships. It's why others continually go back to junk food or a sedentary lifestyle. To do what is good for us, we must change, and change brings up emotional resistance and anxiety.

BE FEARLESS: *We all have a codependent relationship with fear. Once you acknowledge how and why you benefit from being stuck, you can then see long-term and focus on all the reasons why it's better to change than to stay the same.*

I'm sure it's been frustrating for you. I know it is for most of my clients. When they come to me, most of them know they are stuck in a dysfunctional pattern. They don't know why they are stuck, though, and they assume it's because they are not strong enough to break out of it. This couldn't be further from the truth.

What's really going on is something that seems counterintuitive and hard to admit. It's this: they are getting something out of being stuck. They are benefiting from it in some way.

For instance, in Lori's Fear Dump, you can see that she benefits from avoiding going back to school in many ways. By going back to school, she's going to be less comfortable financially and will have to reduce her spending. She'll also have to give up some of her relaxation time in order to balance her roles as parent, wife, and now that of student. Frankly it will be stressful, but it will also be worth it.

BE FEARLESS: *For how long are you willing to settle for second best? How much are you willing to put up with?* *Ask yourself,* When is enough enough?

This codependent relationship is even more apparent in Jake's Fear Dump. He still has fun with his girlfriend and will have to give that up if he breaks up with her. He also still has sex with her. Going without that sex will be yet another downer for him when he breaks things off. And even though she's not right for him, she's still someone. Without her in his life, he'll have to become comfortable with being alone—at least for a while. When I asked him what he was gaining by staying in his dysfunctional relationship, he eventually realized that staying in the relationship helped him to avoid feeling stressed, anxious, and out of his comfort zone.

In Stacy's Fear Dump, you can see the codependent relationship when she talks about not having time and not knowing how to train. Right now she's comfortable. In order to train for a marathon, she'd have to embrace being uncomfortable, at least for a while.

Just like Lori, Jake, and Stacy, you also have a codependent relationship with your fear. The relationship might be subtle and hard to spot, but it's definitely there. It might even be embarrassing. Initially, you might not want to admit it or come to terms with it.

It's for these reasons that I encourage you to have an open mind as you complete the following exercise. Chances are you might not like what you learn. But just sit with it for a while. Over time, I think you will find that the truth will make itself known and will help you to be fearless. Trust me.

Are you ready?

Let's start by taking another look at your Fear Dump. Let's look for all of the things that are going to make you uncomfortable when you confront your fear. Using your Fear Dump, come up with the answers to the following questions:

- How do you benefit from maintaining the status quo?
- What will you gain by continuing to avoid change in your life?
- How will you benefit if your life stays exactly the same?
- What do you gain by doing nothing?
- What do you gain by being stuck?
- Which excuses in the Fear Dump are you benefiting from? Which ones encourage you to stay the same?
- What stress or discomfort would you have to overcome if you were to change your current situation?

Now, based on your results, let's create a Stuck List. On it, list all of the benefits of staying stuck. I know. This is counterintuitive. You might be thinking, *Why do I want to reinforce all of the reasons I want to stay stuck?* This isn't about reinforcing the benefits of staying stuck. It's about identifying them. Only after you identify them and become aware of them can you begin to embrace the necessary short-term stress and discomfort that comes from confronting and overcoming your fear.

Use this Stuck List for guidance and ideas.

Why I Want to Stay Stuck
I get to maintain the status quo. I don't have to confront change.
I avoid the anxiety associated with...
I don't have to get back into the dating or job-hunting world.
I won't have to be lonely.
I won't have to worry about making ends meet.
I won't have to worry about getting rejected.
I won't have to meet new people and put myself out there.

How did you do? Are you feeling a little unsure? Are you questioning what you came up with? Again, sit with it for a bit. Give me the benefit of the doubt for now. There is always something to be gained by giving in to your fear and staying stuck. It's never worth it, mind you, and it's never a reason to not face your fear and not move forward. But it's there, and in order to move forward, you must identify it and deal with it.

Exercise #4: Strengthen Your Payoff List

In order to overcome your Dream Stoppers and your codependent relationship with fear, you'll want to replace the benefits of staying stuck with the stronger, more powerful, and longer-lasting benefits of change. This is easy because you already laid the groundwork in Step 1. Pull out that Payoff List you've already created.

Your Payoff List will help you to end your codependency by helping you to look past the short term—and all the fears and anxieties you've identified in this chapter—and instead see long-term. It will help you to continually remind yourself of what you will eventually gain if you face and move past your fear.

> **BE FEARLESS:** *You can't wish a dream to come true.*
> *You must make it come true.*

Take a look at your list. Can you add more Payoffs? How will your life change when you complete your Dream List? What will you gain by facing your fears and making these dreams a reality for you? How will your life change for the better?

Your Fear Dump helped you to identify why you think you can't, shouldn't, or won't reach this dream. Counter everything from your Fear Dump by listing why you **can**, **should**, and **will** move past this fear. Use the following examples from Lori's, Jake's, and Stacy's Payoff Lists for inspiration in adding to your own.

Lori's Payoff List

I'll be working toward a career I know I'll like.
I'll feel mentally stimulated.
I'll be around like-minded people.
I'll be doing something I feel passionate about.
I'll be happier.
I'll feel better about my marriage.
I'll have balance in my life.
It will teach my husband and me how to problem-solve and come up with creative solutions.

Jake's Payoff List

I'll free myself up so I can create the opportunity to meet someone I'm more compatible with.
I'll be able to settle with someone with whom there's a future.
I'll feel good about being honest to my girlfriend.
I'll feel good knowing I was honest to myself.
I'll gain peace of mind by actually taking action to improve my life.

Stacy's Payoff List

I'll gain a sense of accomplishment.
I'll be in great shape.
I'll tap into strengths and can use them for future endeavors.
I will have found a way to balance my interests with those of my relationship.

Great Job!

You've just completed Step 2 of the five-step plan! By now, fear might be losing some of its hold over you. At the same time, you might be finding that this new way of behaving and thinking is still a little awkward. Many of my clients tell me that the shift from fearful thinking to fearless thinking feels awkward at first. They do, however, get used to it over time. You will too.

To help motivate yourself, I encourage you to create several copies of your Payoff List that you can carry with you in your wallet or purse. Make copies that you can stash at work or at home in strategic locations. Whenever you feel mired by fear and short-term stress, pull out that list and read it. Remind yourself of why you are doing this. Motivate yourself to keep moving forward. Use it as a constant reminder for why you've decided to overcome your fear and why you will continue to pursue your dream.

Fearless Makeover

Frank was stressed out, a problem that stemmed from his perfectionism, a quality that had been instilled in him at an early age. His parents had expected him to be perfect—to get A's in school, excel in sports, be supercourteous and polite, take several languages in school, and so on. Now he was in constant fear of making a mistake.

The Goal: Frank wanted to feel more relaxed, especially at work, and less stressed in general.

The Payoff: If he could reduce his stress, Frank knew he'd have more energy and be able to think more clearly. He'd make better decisions at work, excel in his career, and feel happier.

The Program: In his mind, Frank was either perfect or not (Stopper #3 from Step 2). I told Frank he needed to loosen up his thinking and become comfortable with being messy, making mistakes, and being less than perfect. I gave him a paradoxical prescription. I asked him to, for one week, face his fear of screwing up by actually screwing up on purpose (Step 5). I suggested he arrive late to work, insert grammatical errors into e-mails, wear mismatched clothes, and mess up his perfectly folded towels.

He, of course, pushed back, saying, "I can't do that."

I asked, "Why not? You can always go back to the way you were before."

He said, "I'll get in trouble. I won't get any work done. I'll have to work late to make up the time."

I pushed further. I later learned that they had a flexible start time between 9:00 and 9:30 a.m., but that he usually arrived at work by 8:30 a.m.

"So even if you arrive at work late at 8:45 a.m., you'll still technically be early," I coaxed. By the end of the appointment, he reluctantly agreed to give "being messy" a try.

The following week, he told me that being messy was "anxiety provoking, but I could do it."

The Outcome: Week after week, we continued to shift the norm and help Frank ease into the idea of being messy. Over the course of six sessions, he developed a new standard: less was more. He had found a new range of comfort. He'd loosened up his thinking, was no longer stressed, and had more energy and clarity as a result.

Chapter Eight

Step 3: Rewrite Your Inner Narrative

When John first came to see me for therapy, he was about to see a medical doctor for a prescription. He wasn't interested in a prescription for Xanax or Prozac. Rather, he was convinced he needed Viagra.

"I keep going soft," he almost whispered. "I don't know what's wrong with me."

I knew that John was a healthy fifty-year-old guy, wasn't on any medications, and had no medical issues. He'd even had a physical within the past year and everything was fine. I was pretty sure he didn't need Viagra, but I asked a few questions just to be sure.

Me: "That's normal. It happens to a lot of guys. What makes you think you need Viagra?"

John: "Well it's been going on for a long time. It's getting worse and worse. You don't think I need a prescription?"

Me: "When you masturbate, can you get an erection?"

John: "Yes, no problem."

Me: "Do you ever go soft when you masturbate?"

John: "No."

Me: "What's the difference between sex with yourself and sex with someone else?"

He was stumped.

I explained that apart from the obvious, the difference between the two occurred in his mind, not in his penis. Arousal is arousal, and it's the mind that interprets that sensation.

"I'm pretty sure this is all in your head. Viagra might be able to help an issue in your penis, but it can't fix an issue in your head," I said.

As we talked, I learned that John had first lost his erection about one year before. It happened after a long evening during which he'd consumed a lot of alcohol. It had been a normal enough situation, one that has probably happened to countless men. It would have been an isolated occurrence in John's life had his mind not given it more power.

For John this incident had become a negative reference experience, one that his mind played over and over again. Whenever he attempted to have sex, he remembered the night he had gone soft. Remember, our minds tend to remember negative events first, and these negative memories overshadow the positive ones. The negative memories are more potent, especially if you haven't dealt with them properly. For John this memory brought up fear and anxiety. Whenever he attempted to have intercourse, he thought, *Damn, I have to keep this going. I can't lose this. I better not go soft again! My wife will think less of me if I can't even get it up. She'll find a new lover. I don't know what I am going to do if I can't stay hard. What kind of a man am I?*

He was focusing on everything that he didn't want rather than on what he did want. I knew that this wasn't helping him. When you focus on what you don't want, you tend to make that happen.

Test It Out

Whatever you do, don't think of what a zebra would look like if it had pink and blue stripes. What are you thinking about? I bet you are thinking about a zebra with pink and blue stripes, right? When you try not to think about something, you end up thinking about it even more.

When John told me about the kinds of thoughts that ran through his mind, I said, "Wow, I don't know if I could maintain an erection if that was going through my mind!"

I asked him who his sports heroes are. He mentioned pro basketball player Kobe Bryant and Michael Phelps, the Olympic swimmer who won mega gold in 2008. I asked, "What if every time Kobe got the ball he thought to himself, *I'm no good*, or *I'll never make this basket*? And what if Michael Phelps thought, *I'm so out of shape*, or *There's no way I'm going to win*? How do you think they would perform?" I explained that in both cases, these world-class athletes would not have been able to perform at their level had they injected doubt into their thinking and destabilized their beliefs that they were strong, in great shape, superskilled, and so on.

"You're not any different," I told John. "Every time you get into a situation that could potentially lead to intimacy, your inner narrative is negative, self-defeating, and incompatible with being a confident lover or even feeling good about yourself."

Over time I worked with John, helping him to rewrite the

negative narrative that kept playing in his mind, and eventually he was able to enjoy having sex again rather than fear it.

> **BE FEARLESS:** *Focus on what you want, not on what you don't want. When you focus on what you want, you'll naturally move toward it. Similarly, when you focus on what you don't want, you'll move toward that too. You choose.*

What's Your Narrative?

Like John, we all have an inner narrative that plays in our heads. It's almost like background commentary on what we do and how we feel. These thoughts are constant. You need only to sit quietly and try to not have any thoughts to realize just how many are actually present.

There are lots of theories about where thoughts come from and why. Some of these theories are rooted in religion and spirituality. Over the past few years, some new age theories have popped up about how thoughts are channeled from one person to another, or how vibrations might play a role in creating our thoughts. Some people believe that there's a pool of thoughts out there in the universe that people tap into. The thoughts then pass through you as though you're merely a medium. This approach was strongly promoted by *The Secret* and other books like it. This probably doesn't come as a surprise to you, but I don't support this theory. The problem with it is that it assigns control to some external entity. What good is that going to do you if you're trying to get better, enhance a certain area of your life, or reach peak performance? None!

If you've made it this far, then you probably have a pretty good idea of my style and how I operate and view people. You can probably surmise that I don't give the aforementioned theories much credence. I take a more practical approach, one that is rooted in cognitive science and psychology.

Here's my take: We have an unconscious mind and a conscious mind. The conscious mind is exposed to all sorts of external stimuli such as sensations, sights, smells, flavors, and sounds. The unconscious mind houses deeper memories, thoughts, feelings, and emotions—many of which you may not be aware of during any given moment. Sometimes the stimuli coming in from the conscious mind, however, will trigger a thought or cause an emotion to bubble up from the unconscious. For instance, a few years ago when I was looking for an apartment in Manhattan, I walked into an apartment that had a very distinct smell. The smell reminded me of my grandmother's apartment. It was an old place, just like hers. I mentally drifted off for probably ten seconds as I thought of how I used to sit with her and eat Jell-O or cookies. I thought of how over the years she had become increasingly shakier when pouring hot water for tea. I then thought what she and I might talk about today were she still around. Soon, in my head, I was there with her, telling her about my life and everything she'd missed since she'd passed away.

Just walking into this one apartment had triggered my unconscious mind and a whole range of thoughts and emotions.

I'm sure you've had similar experiences. Maybe you were walking down the street and you saw someone who reminded you of somebody else. Or maybe, like me, a certain smell transported you back to a specific place and time. Whatever it was, it felt as if the thoughts were coming out of nowhere, but they really weren't. They were there all along in the unconscious mind.

It's there where your inner narrative arises. Just because it comes from the unconscious mind, however, doesn't mean you can't become more aware of it, and it doesn't mean you can't rewrite it.

It's not until I point it out to people that they realize just how negative their thoughts are. These negative thoughts are automatic. They're ingrained and as habitual as your morning grooming routine. But just because it's habitual doesn't mean you can't change it. You can break yourself out of the negative thinking that leads to fear, and that's exactly what you will do in this step of the program. You are going to create a new, more positive inner narrative, one that will replace the habitual negative thoughts that, until now, have been triggering your fear response over and over again. In this step of the program, you will rewrite the story that plays over and over in your mind. Right now that story is plotted like a horror film, with one near-death experience after another. After you rewrite the inner narrative, it will read more like a pleasant but believable fairy tale—one with a happily-ever-after.

By rewriting your inner narrative and making it more positive, believable, and encouraging, you will find the fearlessness you need to become the hero of your own story.

Change Your Life in One Week!

Step 3 includes five exercises that will take you roughly one hour to finish over the course of a week. Check them off as you move forward.

☐ **Exercise #1:** Watch your thoughts and become more aware of your negativity. **Estimated time:** 10 to 15 minutes.

☐ **Exercise #2:** Do periodic body scans to gain more insight into your thoughts and feelings. **Estimated time:** 5 to 10 minutes per body scan.

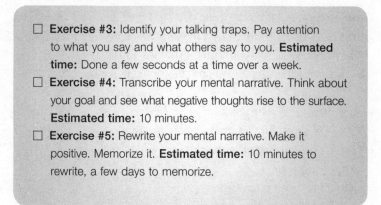

☐ **Exercise #3:** Identify your talking traps. Pay attention to what you say and what others say to you. **Estimated time:** Done a few seconds at a time over a week.

☐ **Exercise #4:** Transcribe your mental narrative. Think about your goal and see what negative thoughts rise to the surface. **Estimated time:** 10 minutes.

☐ **Exercise #5:** Rewrite your mental narrative. Make it positive. Memorize it. **Estimated time:** 10 minutes to rewrite, a few days to memorize.

Exercise #1: Notice Your Thoughts

You might believe, as many people do, that your reactions and feelings are out of your control. This isn't true. Your thoughts and feelings, whether they are conscious or unconscious, are more in your control than you realize.

For instance, that sweaty sensation you get when you are nervous is usually preceded by a thought, one that probably goes something like this, *I can't do this. I can't believe I am trying to do this. I shouldn't even be here. What was I thinking?*

Similarly, the muscle tension you feel when you are under stress is also caused by a thought (or several thoughts). Even those times when you are so scared that your mind seems to go blank, it all started with a thought, one that was fear based.

The problem for most of us, however, is that we are not aware of our own thinking. Consider all of the tasks that you don't remember you do. Did you lock the door when you left this morning? You probably did, because you always do. But do you remember doing it? Probably not. That's because locking the door is an automated response, one that you've done over and over and over again. You don't consciously think *Okay, I'm going to lock the door right now* before you do it. But you think it unconsciously.

Here are other things you probably don't remember doing today:

- Brushing your teeth
- Checking for the mail
- Turning on your computer
- Tying your shoes
- Putting on your socks
- Buttoning your pants

Your negative thoughts are the same. They are there, but you probably don't notice them or remember them. This exercise is designed to help you get in touch with the many thoughts that are in your head at any given moment, conscious and unconscious, positive and negative.

Sit and close your eyes. Bring your attention to your mind. Think of your mind as a screen and your thoughts as the movie playing on that screen. What are you seeing? What are you thinking?

Maybe you are thinking that this is a dumb exercise and you can't believe you are doing it. Good! You just noticed a thought. Or maybe you are thinking that you are going to skip over this exercise because you don't feel like closing your eyes right now. Great, you noticed another thought.

There's no judgment here. It doesn't matter what thoughts you notice. Don't worry about whether they are good thoughts or bad thoughts or about what they mean. Don't analyze them, and don't try to change them. Just notice them.

In your Fearless Notebook, take notes on some of the thoughts you discovered. Then move directly on to Exercise #2 without taking a break.

Fear Antidote: If this exercise was difficult—say you had a hard time noticing a single thought, sensation, or feeling—then try it a few more times over a period of days until you get better at noticing your thoughts.

Exercise #2: Notice Your Feelings and Sensations

Your thoughts often lead to feelings and sensations, but you might not be aware of the connection. For instance, that headache that you get every afternoon might be the result of stressful thoughts you are having about work. Or the sad feeling you have in the evenings might relate to thoughts you have about your marriage but are not aware of.

To make the connection, let's explore how your thoughts produce feelings, emotions, and sensations. You'll do this exercise in two parts.

Part #1. Close your eyes. Zero in on how you feel. Mentally scan your body from head to toe. Are there any areas of tension, discomfort, or pain? Also notice your mood. Are you feeling irritable? Anxious? Bored? Or something else? In your Fearless Notebook, jot down what you've discovered.

Now look at the thoughts you jotted down from Exercise #1. Look at the emotions. How do they fit together?

Part #2. Carry your journal with you. Three to five times a day, take a break from whatever you are doing. Bring your attention to your thoughts. Notice what's going through your mind. Also notice how you feel. Jot it all down. At the end of the week, play detective and see if you can relate your thoughts to your feelings and bodily sensations.

Exercise #3: Identify Your Talking Traps

During the past fifteen years, I've been observing how people talk
and how their language is related to how they think and feel. As
a result, I am often able to pick up on the words and phrases a
client uses over and over again and help the client see how those
words are leading to fear.

The words you use truly are powerful. They can motivate you
to change or they can render you stuck. They can lead you to see
possibilities or into seeing only impossibilities instead.

To understand just how powerful your spoken words really are,
I'd like to share with you a story about a client.

Her name was Donna. Two one-syllable words were causing
her to stay in a dead-end career.

Donna was in her early thirties. She worked hard as an administrative assistant and was well compensated. Her job paid the
bills and allowed her to fund a thriving social life. Her problem,
however, was that she didn't feel fulfilled at all, which, of course,
contributed to her depression. I asked her to think about what
she *really* wanted to do.

As it turned out, Donna felt passionate about fitness and helping others get in shape. She lit up when she talked about fitness,
health, and nutrition.

I asked, "Have you ever considered taking some courses toward
getting certified as a fitness trainer?"

She replied, "**Yeah, but** I could never find the time."

We talked further about how she might find that time. She
figured out that weekend courses would be a viable option.

"Do you think you'd be happy seeing a few clients a week?" I
asked.

"**Yeah, but** how would I do that with my job?"

As we talked, several more *yeah, but*s emerged.

The *yeah, but* talking trap holds many people hostage. I pointed this out to Donna. "Those two words are so powerful," I said. I explained that every *yeah, but* was creating fear, hurting her confidence, and preventing her from taking an important and realistic risk. I pointed out that *yeah, but* was merely an excuse. Donna was hiding behind these words. The language was causing her to focus on all of the why-nots instead of all of the reasons she could, should, and would do something. Every time she got the urge to say "yeah, but," I had her replace the language.

I asked her to keep track of her *yeah, but*s and what time they occurred.

At the following session, she reported that she had ten *yeah, but*s, all during the business day. So at least ten times a day, she dreamed of being in a different career, one that, in her mind, seemed impossible. Eventually she realized it was anything but.

Next to each *yeah, but* in her notebook, we worked together to come up with alternative language that was more motivating and empowering. Here are a few examples of how we rewrote her *yeah, but*s.

"Yeah, But..."	*Yeah, Better*
"Yeah, I want to be a trainer, but I know nothing about personal training."	"I want to be a trainer, so I will go back to school and get my certifications."
"Yeah, I want to be a trainer, but how will I ever balance my schedule with work?"	"I want to be a trainer, and I will balance my schedule by being creative and flexible."
"Yeah, I want to be a trainer, but how will I build my clientele?"	"I will market myself to large apartment buildings."

Donna went on to make the impossible possible, and now she is one of the most sought-after trainers in New York City. I recently checked in with her and asked her, "A few years ago, if I told you that you would be doing this for a living full-time, what would you have said?"

Without much thought she said, "Yeah, but."

I'd love to have you come in for a session, listen to you talk, and point out your talking traps for you. This obviously isn't realistic, though. Therefore I'd like to help you identify your talking traps by taking Exercises #1 and #2 a bit farther. Carry your Fearless Notebook with you for a few days and take note of the following:

1. The moments when you feel yourself tensing up with fear, anxiety, or stress; and try to pinpoint the language you used just before you tensed up.

2. The negative language used by others around you; and see how that language relates to the choices they make every day. Study the people around you. What types of words do they use? Do they repeat certain words and phrases? What body language and facial expressions and tone do they use to voice those words? Are their words empowering or negative? Are there common themes?

At the end of the week, look over your journal and see if you can spot any trends. Specifically, look for the following:

The negative and demotivating statements made by others around you. Make the connection between the negativity and how it affects their lives. What kinds of people made these statements? Are they happy and confident people? Or are they fearful and angry people? Are they the kinds of people who go for and get what they want in life? Or are they the kinds of people who never seem to get what they want? What are the words that people use? Are these words perpetuating or defusing their fear, anger, and depression?

Words or phrases that tend to come up over and over again for you. Are there any common themes? What words and phrases seem habitual for you? What are your *yeah, but* ticks?

Words and phrases that tend to send you into a negative loop. What causes your negative thoughts to reinforce themselves?

Fear Antidote: Initially, as you attempt to do this exercise, you might feel challenged or frustrated. Maybe you might capture some of your language but can't capture the feelings you are having at any given moment. Other times you might capture the feelings, but you can't remember the language. That's okay. Go easy on yourself. Take a few days to do this exercise. I want you to have enough time to practice and perfect the technique of noticing your language and how it relates to your feelings and daily choices. Eventually you will become more aware of your thinking, language, feelings, and actions. Trust me.

Exercise #4: Transcribe Your Mental Narrative

Until now, you've been working on identifying your negativity in a general way. Now it's time to pinpoint a specific set of negative thoughts—the very ones that are standing between you and the goal you wish to accomplish.

For instance, when I counseled John, his goal was simple. He wanted to have reliable erections. His negative narrative centered on how he felt about himself for not being able to maintain an erection and it sounded like this:

- *What kind of a man can't get it up with his wife?*
- *I've lost my manhood.*

- *I'm old.*
- *Something is seriously wrong with me.*
- *My wife will leave me.*

No wonder he was having issues in the bedroom!

Like John, you also have a negative narrative playing in your head, and this narrative is standing between you and your goal. Before you rewrite it, you first must locate it, listen to it, and understand it.

To find and listen to the narrative, visualize yourself going through the motions of accomplishing your dream. For instance, I had John go home and think about having sex with his wife. I asked him to make it vivid and comprehensive. I asked him to close his eyes and see, feel, hear, and touch everything in that moment. "What would it look like? What would it feel like? What would it smell like?" I asked. These questions helped him to associate himself into the experience and made it as real as possible.

Like John, I'd like you to see yourself accomplishing your goal. What does it look like when you do it? What does it sound like? What does it feel like?

Don't worry about manipulating the outcome just yet. Just uncover the unconscious narrative for now. Think about what you want to accomplish. Maybe you are thinking about asking that special someone out on a date. Or maybe you visualize being assertive with your spouse or asking your boss for a raise. Whatever it is, bring it to mind.

As you think about your dream, thoughts will bubble up. What are they? Are they negative in nature? What are they telling you to do or not to do? How do they make you feel?

Jot these thoughts and feelings down in your Fearless Notebook. Then move on to Exercise #5.

Exercise #5: Rewrite Your Narrative

Now that you've identified the negative narrative associated with your dream, it's time to transform it into one that's more motivating.

With John, for instance, I worked to help him to see that his penis did not define his self-worth. For starters, I asked him to define sex.

"Getting my wife off," he said.

It's not surprising that his sense of self was so shattered with thinking like that. He imposed such rigid standards on himself and pressure by seeing sex merely as a way to bring his wife to orgasm. His penis was directly connected to his ego, and sadly his ego and sense of self was determined by his penis. This is common. With a lot of men, their egos are tied to their penises. So, if the penis is performing, then they feel like a million bucks, whereas if it isn't, then they feel quite the opposite and it can lead to depression, low confidence, and, with John, performance issues.

"What about the experience of simply being with your wife?" I asked.

John looked dumbfounded. Like a lot of men, he was narrowly focused on his genitals and hers, while neglecting the rest of the body. I explained to John that the whole body is potentially orgasmic, or at minimum can feel really good. Over time John was able to redefine sex and make it all-encompassing to include simply being close to his wife, intimate kisses, holding each other, cuddling, and so on. He was able to eliminate his rigid thinking and expand his sexual horizons.

I asked John to come up with words that describe a good lover. He came up with *confident*, *assertive*, *sensitive*, and *affectionate*. He also said a good lover would know what his wife liked and be familiar with her needs in bed.

We then examined expectations. He expected to bring her to mind-blowing, earth-shattering orgasms each and every time and he thought she expected that too—a belief that proved untrue.

I then instructed John to forget he had a penis and that his wife had a vagina. It was a difficult task, I know. I encouraged him to find new ways to be close to his wife and share the experience. I challenged him to find new ways to excite his wife.

We also worked on how he spoke to himself. I had John then create a chart. On one side, he listed all of the negative phrases that tended to go through his mind when he was having sex with his wife. On the other, I asked him to reframe those thoughts to something more positive, more motivating, and more likely to give him the confidence he needed to relax and get an erection. This is what his chart looked like:

My Negative Narrative	*My Positive Narrative*
You're not a real man.	I am strong and virile.
If I can't keep it up, I don't know what I will do.	Every part of her body and mine is potentially arousing and orgasmic.
I'm despicable.	I'm super-sexy.
I'm a sorry excuse for a man.	I'm confident and strong.
I'm weak.	Blood is pumping through my body and supplying energy to my muscles.
I'm a bad lover.	I'm crazy about my wife.
I'm boring in bed.	I'm wild and exciting.

After creating the chart, the challenge was for him to notice the negative thoughts when they popped up and to immediately replace them with the positive ones from the chart. In just a few sessions, John was able to move past his fear and maintain an erection—without the help of medications.

Now it's time for you to rewrite your own narrative. For help, consult the examples below. They include sample negative and positive narratives for several goals and dreams.

Negative Narratives	Positive Narratives
Narrative About Asking for a Raise	
I'll never get a raise.	I'll never know if I can get a raise unless I ask.
The company doesn't have money.	I'm a valuable employee who is vitally important to this company.
My boss doesn't like me.	Where's the evidence to support this thought? Have I ever asked my boss what he thinks of me?
I'll stumble on my words.	I'll prepare for this experience in a thoughtful way.
Narrative About Buying a Car	
I know nothing about cars.	I'm a good consumer.
I'll get ripped off.	I'm smart with my money.
I feel intimidated by salespeople.	I'm confident and resourceful.

continued

Negative Narratives	Positive Narratives
I'll feel guilty if I take up the salesperson's time and end up not buying this car.	This is how business works and it's this person's job to help me.
Narrative About Applying for Work	
I'll never find a job.	I'm working hard to find a job.
Companies don't like me.	The right fit exists. I'll find it.
I feel like an outcast around my friends.	This is a tough economy. I'm not alone.
I'm going to be out on the street if I don't find a job.	I have a strong support network and no one is going to let me go hungry and be homeless.

How to Memorize Your New Narrative

Many years ago, I left a message for a TV producer pertaining to a project I was working on. When he called back he offered me this unsolicited advice, "Look Jonathan, you left a one-minute message and in just one minute, I counted twenty *um*s. You've got to change that."

At the time I wasn't even aware of all of the *um*s in my speech, just as you probably were not aware of your negative thinking until you did the exercises in this chapter. Once that producer made me aware of it, however, I set out to drop my *um*s.

It wasn't easy.

Talking without my *um*s felt foreign to me at first, almost clumsy. I felt as if my attempts were flat and forced. I had a really hard time catching myself.

I eventually enlisted the help of friends and family. I asked them, "Can you point out whenever you notice me saying, 'um'? I'm trying not to say it anymore, but I'm having a hard time. I could use some help."

They did, and it was tough but I eventually changed. With this constant reinforcement, I eventually dropped the *ums* from my language.

It's going to be the same with you and your positive narrative. Knowing what you want to tell yourself is one thing. Actually remembering to do it is another.

It will take lots of practice to memorize your new narrative. You are used to thinking in a negative, demotivating way. It's a bad habit. As you attempt to reframe your thoughts, the process will feel uncomfortable and foreign to you. Please trust the process and keep practicing. The more you practice, the better you will get at it. Eventually it won't feel so forced. Many of my clients find it awkward at first, but as with many things they eventually get used to it. Have you ever come from the dentist after getting a filling? At first it feels weird. Then a week or two later you don't even notice it. It will be the same with your positive narrative. You'll eventually get used to it.

Initially you might not even believe the positive statements you are telling yourself. That's okay. Just fake it until you make it, as the saying goes. Mentally say the motivating thoughts to yourself. Eventually you really will believe them.

Also enlist the help of your Fearless Support Team. Give your support team your list of negative and positive statements. Ask your team members to point out when they notice you talking in the negative.

Over time and with practice, you will start catching yourself and reframing your thoughts without consciously trying to do it. You will get better and better at it. Eventually you will catch yourself midthought, just as my clients do, and you will be able to reframe them right away. After that you will even naturally have positive thoughts without having to reframe them at all.

Fearless Makeover

Michelle was fearful of riding the subway. She'd tried antianxiety medication without success and came to me as her last resort. She interpreted noises—a screech, a rattle, a bump—as impending doom.

The Goal: To ride the subway without fear and anxiety.

The Payoff: If she overcame her fear of the subway, Michelle could cut an hour off her work commute.

The Program: I told Michelle we needed to reprogram her thinking and redefine the meaning of these cues. A noise, a bump, the announcer saying there's a slight delay and so on were not signs of danger and disaster. On the New York subway, these things are routine.

I asked Michelle to write her beliefs about the subway on one side of a page. On the other side, we worked at reframing them to more realistic and more positive statements (Step 3). So, for example, Michelle had equated the door closing with doom. Her more positive reframe was, "Good, the door is closing as it should. The train is operating as it should, and we're moving closer to our destination in an efficient way."

Then we met near the subway station and sat at a bench. I noticed Michelle getting nervous. Her breathing became shallow, her face seemed tense, and she was withdrawn. I taught

Michelle some relaxation techniques (Step 4), and then I asked her if she would simply walk down the stairs (Step 5).

We walked down the stairs and looked at a subway map. I asked her to show me where she lived, where she worked, and the subway lines that would take her to and from work.

We heard noises from the tracks. Michelle grew tense. I asked her to think about what else those noises might mean, such as normal machinery coming to a stop, metal on metal, and doors opening and closing. We stayed in the station for twenty minutes so she could hear the same noises a few times. She left feeling optimistic and proud of her accomplishment. She hadn't been inside of a subway station in eight years!

For homework, I asked Michelle to enter the subway station near her home during the week and do the same thing: stand in the station for twenty minutes and reprogram what the noises meant to her. She did this over and over until she could enter a station and feel calm.

The Outcome: When it came time to ride the train, Michelle was tense, but not to the point where she wanted to flee. She was like a kid who was learning to ride a bicycle for the first time and notices her dad no longer has a hand on the seat. On the platform I asked Michelle to visualize success. In her mind, she watched herself make each step that she needed to take to reach her goal of making a successful trip. We got on the train. Michelle continuously redefined and reevaluated the noises she heard. We had a slight delay, and Michelle was even able to see that delays were normal. She made it! Michelle's next assignment was to ride the subway with a friend and then, eventually, alone. Within just a few weeks, she was able to completely overcome her fear.

Chapter Nine

Step 4: Eliminate Your Fear Response

Many years ago when I was just out of graduate school, I worked in a hospital emergency department in a small blue-collar mill town in Connecticut. There I counseled hundreds of patients who were psychotic, gravely depressed, suicidal, and addicted to drugs and alcohol. My responsibility was to evaluate them and determine the best course of treatment.

Some of these patients checked in to the ER with disorders such as schizophrenia and, at the time I counseled them, were hearing voices and seeing things that were not really there. As you might imagine, they felt confused, overwhelmed, stressed, and scared.

Most of all, they felt out of control.

Of the hundreds of such patients I counseled, one really stood out. I'll never forget the sight of her. The police brought her to the ER after she stabbed her pet cat to death. She was a sweet, fragile-looking, white-haired granny with blood on her hands. I felt both sad and scared for her. What if her two grandchildren had been visiting her? What if she had been babysitting them? Would she have gone on to stab them too?

I asked, "Why did you do this?"

She said, "The voices told me to do it."

"Do you hear those voices now?" I asked.

"Yes," she said, adding that they were lingering in the background.

On a hunch, I asked her, "That's interesting. Can you make the voices louder?"

She looked at me as if I were the person who was crazy. She seemed stunned actually. I could only surmise that she'd never been asked such a question. She sat quietly with a deep, pensive look on her face. I could tell something was going on.

I asked her to imagine a knob on a radio that controls the volume. "Imagine you're turning the knob slightly clockwise to make the sound a bit louder."

She did just that. I asked her to continue to make them louder, all while knowing she was safe in the hospital (and so was I). She did.

I could see her face showing more and more distress, yet strangely she seemed to have more control.

"If you can make them louder, then you can probably make them quieter too," I said. "Want to try it?"

She nodded.

I motioned with my hand for her to turn the knob slightly counterclockwise.

She did and had a look of fascination on her face.

We went back and forth. She turned up the volume on her voices. Then she turned it down. She turned it up. Then down again, over and over.

This seemingly simple exercise was powerful. It gave her control over something that she thought she had no control over. She thought the voices controlled her. As it turned out, she could control the voices. She just didn't know it.

Now, this exercise certainly wasn't a cure, but it was definitely a way for this woman to cope. Probably for the first time, she felt that she actually had some control over her demons.

I'm telling you this story not because I think you can identify with what it's like to hear voices that aren't really there. But I do think you might be able to identify with the sensation of being out of control. Have you ever felt as if your body's reaction to stress, fear, and anxiety was uncontrollable? Many of my clients tell me they feel this way. They use phrases like "There's nothing I can do about it" and "My body just reacts. I can't stop it." When it's really severe, they feel as if they are separate from their bodies, as if they are floating outside of themselves and watching their bodies freak out. This is dissociation. It's the body's way of protecting itself under extreme stress and trauma. This is one of the wonders of the mind, and it causes many people to disconnect and feel out of control of their fear response also. It's adaptive, protective even.

As it turns out, however, you are in control. Just as several of my schizophrenic patients learned how to manipulate the voices in their heads, you can alter how your body responds to stress. For instance, you really do have some control over:

- Whether or not your hands or arms tremble
- Whether or not your voice shakes
- Whether or not your mind goes blank
- Whether or not your palms sweat
- Whether or not your heart feels as if it is pounding out of your chest

Many of these responses are automatic. Your heart beats without you telling it to beat. You sweat without consciously thinking about it. It's the same with blushing. But you still have some control over these automatic responses. You might not be able to stop them or eliminate them, but you can make them less intense. It might not seem like it right now, but it's true. You blush, for instance, when you are nervous. While you can't mentally force the pinkness out of your face, you *can* relax the nerves that caused the blushing in the first place, and, in turn, get that pinkness to subside. The mind-body connection is undeniably strong.

It's important for you to know that these sensations are actually more in your control than you may realize. Your body is not the boss of you. You are the boss of your body. In this chapter, you are going to learn a simple exercise that will prove this to you and help you to gain control. You will also create and practice a Fear Response Strategy that you can use to calm yourself as needed.

More important than getting in control of the fear response, however, is this: the fear response can actually be helpful. It can work in your favor rather than against you. In this step of the program, you will learn not only how to control the fear response—by slowing that racing heartbeat at will—but you will also learn how to use the fear response to drive you forward, fuel you with energy and motivation, and give you the extra advantage you need to succeed at anything you attempt. By the end of this chapter, you will no longer fear the fear. You won't panic when you feel your heart thumping in your chest or your palms getting sweaty. Rather you will know it's normal, why it's happening, what to do about it, and how to use it as a strength. Let's get started.

Change Your Life in One Week!

Step 4 includes six exercises that don't take very long to try but must be repeated and done over time to master. They are all very simple and, much like brushing your teeth, can easily be incorporated into your life. Make sure to do Exercises #2 and #3 back to back without a break.

☐ **Exercise #1:** Prove to yourself that no one is immune to fear. Everyone feels it. Watch and talk to other people. Do some research on the Internet to identify celebrities who have anxiety, phobias, or stage fright. **Estimated time:** 30 minutes.

☐ **Exercise #2:** Get yourself as anxious as possible. **Estimated time:** 10 minutes.

☐ **Exercise #3:** Get yourself as calm as possible. Practice a relaxation method every day. (See the simple one we present in the section "How to Relax" in Exercise 3 of this chapter.) **Estimated time:** 10 minutes a day.

☐ **Exercise #4:** Find ways to turn your fear into a strength. **Estimated time:** 15 minutes.

☐ **Exercise #5:** Create your Fear Response Strategy. Use it whenever you are headed into a tense situation. **Estimated time:** 10 to 15 minutes.

☐ **Exercise #6:** Reduce the stress in your life. **Estimated time:** 10 minutes to think of stress-reducing options.

Exercise #1: Normalize Your Fear Response

We fear what we don't understand.

It's for this reason that most people fear the fear response more than they fear the situations that trigger it. What goes through many people's heads isn't necessarily *This audience is going to eat me alive* or *She's going to reject me* (although there is definitely some of that too, and you will learn how to deal with it in Step 3). What really gets people in a panic are thoughts like this:

Oh my. My palms are sweating. This isn't good.
I'm sweating and this is a catastrophe. My shirt is drenched.
  I'm trembling.
Oh no! My hands are shaking. She's going to notice and this is
  terrible and I can't make it stop and I'm so out of control
  and oh my now they are shaking even worse!
I can feel my face turning red. I can't stop this. Everyone is
  staring at me. This is so embarrassing.

When you have thoughts like this, they create even more fear that only serves to reinforce the initial fear—making it stronger and even more debilitating.

This is true of *any* sensation, not just anxiety. For instance, I tend to get migraine headaches. In the past, when I would get an aura—the blurred vision that is a sign of a migraine to come—it would freak me out. I would become upset, anxious, and panicky, thinking thoughts like, *Oh, no! I don't have time to have a migraine! This is terrible! What am I going to do?*

These thoughts led to anxiety and fear, which in turn led to muscle tension—muscle tension that made the migraine even worse. I now know to shift my thinking as soon as the first hints of an impending headache set in. I tell myself, *I might be getting a migraine. Sure this sucks, but it won't kill me. I'll recover. I've gotten through this before and I will get through this again.*

This allows me to take back some control. As a result the experience of having a migraine isn't as bad as it would have been had I panicked.

Similarly, several years ago a physician diagnosed me with slightly elevated blood pressure. The diagnosis didn't make much sense. Here I was, a young, skinny, healthy guy. I didn't smoke. I ate healthy. I was the last person you'd expect to have high blood pressure. Still, I took the diagnosis seriously. I took blood-pressure-lowering medication and began monitoring my pressure often in an attempt to pinpoint what was causing it to spike.

The problem was that I began anticipating a negative reading, and this became a self-fulfilling prophecy for me. The more I anticipated the bad reading, the higher my pressure rose.

It was only after I got a second opinion from another doctor who told me that my pressure was normal and just runs slightly higher than others that I realized that it was my anticipatory thoughts that were causing the pressure to spike!

It's the same with your fear response. You might start out with a normal, benign and *very common* physiological reaction. That reaction causes you, however, to think a series of thoughts that heighten the reaction, creating a vicious cycle.

Does this sound familiar? I bet it does. The vast majority of people fear the fear more than they fear anything else. To them the fear response—a racing heartbeat, blushing, a dry mouth, and more—is scarier than change, commitment, ridicule, criticism, failure, and much more.

This was true for me for years, and it was also true of the majority of the people I've counseled as well as several friends and colleagues. It's normal to fear what you do not understand. Remember, uncertainty breeds anxiety. We don't know how the story will end, so we fill in the blanks by making up an ending—one that is usually scarier than what is actually happening to us in real life.

That's why, in this initial exercise, you are going to combat the fear with one of the most potent fear antidotes around: knowledge. By the end of this exercise, you will understand how and why your body reacts to fear. This will help you to normalize that reaction and help break you out of the fear response cycle.

As I've mentioned, your fear response is left over from a time when these sensations worked to keep us alive. Your fear response is really just a physiological reaction designed to keep you alive when you are in the face of a threat. For our ancestors, it served a purpose. It saved their lives.

We rarely confront wild animals in modern times, but the fear response remains and it primes us to run or fight, even when these responses are not in our best interest. For instance you don't want to run from a networking event, and you don't want to punch the person you are attempting to exchange business cards with either. That's why many people default to the third instinctual option: they freeze.

They don't ask for the raise. They don't ask that cutie out on a date. They don't press Send on the online job application. They don't confront a spouse about a dicey issue.

They ignore. They get stuck. They do nothing.

Until now, that is. The old you ignored, got stuck, and did nothing. The new you will use the fear response to move into action.

What's most important for you to understand about your fear response is this: it's all in your head. That's what gives you the control.

Yes, the fear response might get triggered without your consent. You might notice yourself feeling anxious and think, *I did not turn this on. My body is doing this all by itself.*

In reality, however, you did turn on the response, and you turned it on with a thought—one that was fearful and negative in nature. You turned it on with a thought like:

Everyone is going to think what I have to say is stupid.
She's just going to laugh at me.
I can't do this.

My boss is going to fire me.
He'll think I'm fat.
I can't satisfy my wife.
I'm going to lose my erection.
I'm going to forget what I am supposed to say at the meeting.

In Step 3 you learned how to gain control over such thinking so you can stop or weaken the fear response before it starts. And by this step, you will learn how to weaken your fear response even more.

This starts with understanding that fear is normal, expected, and probably not a big deal. Normalizing your response is crucial. It's the thought that you are abnormal that is adding strength to the fear response.

It's the same with any negative emotion. For instance, when I have clients who have just lost a loved one, they are very upset and distraught. I always tell them, "This is normal. If you didn't feel distraught, it wouldn't be normal." As soon as I say those words I can tell they feel a little bit better. By telling themselves that they were too sad or too emotional, they were strengthening the very emotion they wanted to weaken.

Everyone feels fear. You are not the only person who does. If you didn't feel fear, you would be abnormal! For instance, I've told you some about the great basketball player Michael Jordan. Did you know that he openly admits to feeling nervous before most of his games?

That's just one example. I could have listed dozens. If you'd like, search online for the following famous people along with the word *fear* and see what comes up. I think you'll be surprised at just how common nerves really are:

- Whoopi Goldberg
- Jennifer Aniston

- Marilyn Monroe
- Sheryl Crow
- Howie Mandel
- Madonna
- Aretha Franklin
- Justin Timberlake
- Kim Basinger
- Donny Osmond
- Harrison Ford

The list goes on.

But don't stop there. I want you to go out and find more. Gain more examples of just how normal fear is by casually talking to friends and family and coworkers about fear and nervousness. For instance, you might ask questions like:

- Do you ever wonder what other people might think of you?
- Do you ever worry that you might be judged?
- Do you worry that people think you are incompetent or stupid?
- Do you ever get nervous before you _____?

The more examples you have the better, because I want you to eventually tell yourself whenever you feel fear: *This is normal. This is just my body getting prepared. The extra blood pumping through my body right now is good for me. This is normal and beneficial. If I didn't feel this way, I wouldn't be normal.*

This exercise probably seems deceptively simple. Yet normalizing your fear response is actually quite powerful. Just understanding that you are not alone, not a freak, and not abnormal will go a long way toward helping you to take back some control.

But you need more. You need proof—proof that you can actually control these sensations rather than be controlled by them.

So let's give you some control. To prove it to you, let's move on to Exercise #2.

Exercise #2: Prove That You Have Control over Your Fear Response

In my practice I often tell my clients to go ahead and get really anxious and intensify it as much as they can. It's a paradoxical and perhaps an even completely unorthodox recommendation, but the exercise helps prove to them that—like the cat lady I described earlier in this chapter—they really do have control over something that usually happens unconsciously.

I'm going to ask you to do the same. This exercise might go against your sense of logic and everything that you feel is rational. Please bear with me. I'm suggesting you do this for a good reason. If I hadn't seen so many of my clients see such dramatic results with this exercise, I wouldn't keep recommending it.

I want you to get yourself as anxious as you can. To do so sit down, close your eyes, and think about a situation that would normally make you anxious and fearful. Perhaps it's getting in front of a large group of people and speaking, or maybe it's going on the dance floor. Try to imagine every detail of this fear-inducing situation that you can. Use all of your senses. See it, hear it, taste it, feel it, touch it.

If you can't think of an anxiety-provoking scenario from your life, then use the one that follows. It's completely made up, but it should still get the fear response going.

Imagine that you are walking down a street in a desolate

section of a city. It's dark and it's very late at night. All of the shops are closed. There's no one around. You hear footsteps behind you. The footsteps are getting louder and louder. Now you can hear heavy breathing. You actually feel the presence of someone behind you. There's the sensation of a cool blade against your neck.

What's going on in your body? If you are like most of my clients, you might notice that your heart is thumping in your chest. Your palms might be sweaty. Your entire body might feel tense.

That's your fear response kicking in.

Good. Now intensify it. Make yourself ten times more anxious than you would normally become in such a situation. For instance, if you are imagining a speech from your own life, instead of ten eyes looking at you, now there are forty eyes. They are staring at you with an intense gaze. Your heart is pounding even faster. You are sweating, and it shows on your shirt. You are being called upon, and you feel bombarded with questions. People look like they are upset with you.

Make it really vivid. What would that feel like to you? Think about how your body normally responds when you are fearful, and create that reaction. Clench your jaw. Tighten your muscles. Take short and shallow breaths. Squeeze your fists.

How is that for you? Are you really super-tense?

Good!

And don't worry. I'll teach you how to reverse all of this tension very soon. For now give yourself a pat on the back. This exercise took courage. You have more bravery than you realize.

More important, you just proved a piece of vital information to yourself—a piece of information that you would have doubted if you had not completed this exercise. You just gained control over something that usually occurs unconsciously. You manipulated your fear response. You just turned it on all by yourself—even though there was nothing around to trigger it. You also intensified it all by yourself.

You really do have some control over it, don't you? I don't want you feeling this anxious and tense for much longer though, so move directly on to Exercise #3 to find out how to turn the dial in the opposite direction.

Fear Antidote: Did you have a hard time with this exercise? Were you unable to make yourself tense? This might be because you either are scared of the exercise or you have a difficult time with visualization. In either case, what you can do instead is put yourself in a real-life situation that would normally make you nervous and uncomfortable, then attempt to magnify the discomfort. Either way, once you've proven that you can control your stress response, it's time to learn how to turn it off.

Exercise #3: Gain Control over Your Fear Response

Many people attempt to gain control of their fear response with outside help. They take anti-anxiety medications before a speech or they chug a beer before a date.

I'm going to teach you how to reduce the fear response without medication and without alcohol.

It's all very simple. In the previous exercise, you tensed yourself up by activating your sympathetic nervous system. The sympathetic nervous system is the origin of the fear response. It's the nervous system that your body relies on for alertness, strength, and speed.

Your nervous system actually has two parts, though. You also have a parasympathetic nervous system—the nervous system responsible for clarity, calm, collectedness, and relaxation. Just as you used a simple visualization exercise to turn on your sympathetic nervous system (the fear response), you'll use another exercise to turn on the parasympathetic system. It's called Progressive Muscle Relaxation (PMR) and it's no more complicated than tensing and releasing the muscles in your body. You see, the fear response is triggered and strengthened, in part, by muscle tension. That's why you tend to get a headache, neckache, or backache after experiencing a bout of anxiety or fear.

Right now your muscles are probably tenser than you realize. Your muscles maintain this tension at all times, so you become used to it and don't even realize that they are so tense. It's similar to living in a location where there is low-level noise 24/7. For instance, I live in New York City, where the noise of traffic is constant. No matter where I find myself, I am greeted with the sound of sirens, horns, and constant chatter. It's so constant that I don't even notice it. It's not until I leave New York City, go away for a few days, and then come back that I realize how noisy it is here.

Muscle tension is similar to the noise of the city. Even though you are not consciously aware of it, it's still affecting you and it leads to headaches, backaches, high blood pressure, and other chronic problems.

Test It Out

Do you have a close friend or loved one who is naturally cool, calm, and collected—someone who exudes a zen-like serene quality? If so, ask if you can press into his or her muscles. Maybe you even give this person a quick shoulder massage. What you will notice is that his or her muscles are soft and pliable—much like bread dough. Then touch your own. If you are highly fearful, you'll probably find that your muscles are hard, tight, and tense to the touch.

In order to relax your muscles, you will first tense them up even more. This extra tension serves as a physical trigger that allows you to relax. It's similar to pulling your shoulders up as high as they can possibly go and then dropping them.

Once you relax your muscles, you trigger your parasympathetic nervous system to kick on—and once it kicks on, the fear response switches off. This helps to lower levels of stress hormones—in turn reducing blood pressure, heart rate, blood sugar, sweating, and more.

How to Relax

To do Progressive Muscle Relaxation (PMR) sit or lie comfortably, somewhere you feel safe and where you will not be interrupted. Then tense and release the following muscle groups, starting with your head and moving down, systemically, to your feet.

- **Forehead and scalp:** Wrinkle your brow, bringing your eyebrows together as if you are angry. Try to make the skin on your scalp as tight as a drum. Hold for five seconds. Release so that your forehead and scalp feel as if warm wet spaghetti noodles are draped over them.
- **Eyes and nose:** Squeeze your eyes shut. Hold for five seconds. Release.
- **Lips and jaw:** Tighten your jaw and lips as if you were trying to look mean and scary, gritting and baring your teeth. Hold for five seconds and then release, dropping your jaw all the way and softening all of your facial muscles.
- **Shoulders:** Shrug them up to your ears. Hold five seconds. Release and imagine yourself dropping them all the way to the floor.
- **Arms:** Hold your arms tight and straight against your body. Then release them.

- **Hands:** Clench your hands into fists. Hold for five seconds. Release.
- **Upper back:** Pull your shoulder blades together. Hold five seconds. Release.
- **Back:** Arch and tighten your back. Hold five seconds. Release.
- **Stomach:** Tighten your stomach muscles. Release.
- **Hips:** Squeeze your hips and butt. Hold five seconds. Release.
- **Thighs:** Tighten your thighs. Hold five seconds. Release.
- **Feet:** Scrunch up your feet and curl your toes. Hold five seconds. Release.

How do you feel? Relaxed? Good! You've just proven to yourself that you can not only create the fear response at will, but you can weaken it, too. (Note: if Progressive Muscle Relaxation failed to work for you, then try one of the alternative relaxation strategies mentioned in the Fear Antidote on page 209).

Now here's the thing. You want to be able to bring on this state of relaxation at any time and especially during a fearful situation. For that to happen, you'll need to practice it a lot.

I recommend you practice PMR at least once every day. After every session, scan your body and try to memorize the sensation of being relaxed. Start your practice sessions in calming, non-threatening locations, like at home. Over time progress to more stressful situations, such as the office. Eventually, try to bring on this state of relaxation wherever you find yourself—and without tensing your muscles first.

Use these pointers when practicing PMR:

- Practice on a schedule. This will help you remember to do it.
- Do it when you feel alert. Too many people decide to relax just before bed, so they fall asleep. This is great if you

want to use PMR as a tool that helps you fall asleep, but not so great if you are trying to use it to override your fear response. You want to do it while you are alert so you can study it, memorize it, and use it on cue.

- Do it even if you think you are feeling great. Many of my clients don't realize how tense they are until they do the PMR exercise. They think, *I don't need to relax. I'm fine.* Then they do the exercise and realize just how tense they really were. I'm guessing you will be similar.

Fear Antidote: Some people have trouble relaxing with PMR. Are you one of them? If so, all is not hopeless. You just need to try out a few other strategies until you find one that works for you. Here are a few to experiment with:

- **Deep breathing:** When we feel fearful, we tend to breathe rapidly and shallowly. Deep breathing reverses this, helping to turn off the fear response. As you inhale, try to fully expand your midsection. Bring the air first to the very bottom of your lungs by bringing your tummy outward. Then expand your rib cage to the sides. Finally expand your collarbones. Then let it all go. Repeat.

- **Visualization:** Close your eyes and imagine yourself somewhere you have felt happy and relaxed in the past. Maybe it's a warm beach or the cool mountains or somewhere else. Pick a specific location, a place you've been to and felt happy, at ease, content, and comfortable. Visualize every detail of being in this place—how it feels, how it smells, how it looks, and how it sounds.

- **Mindfulness:** The goal here is to completely bring your mind into the present moment. By doing so, you relax without really trying. Sit or lie. Close your eyes. Bring your attention to your breathing. Notice the cool sensation at the ends of your nostrils as you inhale and the warm sensation at the ends of your nostrils as you exhale. Feel your rib cage expand as you inhale and relax as you exhale. In lieu of being mindful of your breathing, you can also try being completely mindful of an activity. For instance, as you walk, notice the sensation of your feet as they touch and lift off the ground. Or if you are washing dishes, pay close attention to the sensation of warm, soapy water on your hands.

Exercise #4: Turn Your Fear into a Strength

Let's get to one of the most powerful exercises in this chapter. Let's learn how to use the fear response to your advantage.

Most people think of the fear response as a negative thing. They want to eliminate it. They can't see how it could ever be helpful.

But in many cases it really can be helpful.

Think about how your body reacts when you are fearful. What happens? What sensations do you notice? What goes through your mind? Does your heart race? Do you blush? Do you sweat? Does your mouth go dry? Do you feel as if you will lose your bowels?

Think about why your body might be reacting in this way. What is your body attempting to do? Could there be any hidden benefit to this reaction? One you could adapt to and use to your advantage? If you did not fear your fear response and didn't feel the need to completely eliminate it, would any of it be useful to you? Doesn't the alertness that comes from the fear response help you to think more clearly and quickly? Or does the increased heart rate give you more energy—energy you can use to drive you forward?

For instance, when I was on CNN's *Nancy Grace* show I felt

my heart pounding really hard. Most hosts or reporters want to make their expert guests look good because doing so adds to the story. Nancy Grace though is known for being antagonistic with her expert guests. I know a few experts who refuse to go on her show for that very reason. I thought, *Do I really need this stress?*

My fearless response: *No, I don't, but it's good for me and could lead to more opportunities.*

Despite that early eagerness and enthusiasm, I still found myself sitting in her studio on live national TV with great anticipation and fear. My heart was pounding through my chest. My muscles were filled with blood and tense. I was breathing heavy. I felt as if I were going into battle. In a way I was. I anticipated being attacked and discredited by the host so naturally my body and mind had to prepare.

I found it comforting to know that my body was doing what it was supposed to be doing so automatically. During a commercial I took a few seconds to settle down. I did a quick inventory of my body. My pounding heart was due to the release of adrenaline, a hormone that prepares the body for action. My dry mouth was due to fluids moving to other parts of my body. Simply reminding myself of the normalcy of these sensations helped. I then imagined myself lying on a raft in a gentle body of water. I was rocking ever so gently with the waves. This helped to calm me. Then I took the sensations that remained and I used them to my advantage. They became the extra focus and energy I needed to really be on when it was my turn to talk.

For you to turn your fear response into a strength, I'd like you to make a list of all of the ways your body tends to respond to stress, anxiety, and fear. Then think about ways that you might be able to use these responses to your advantage. Use the chart that follows for ideas:

Symptom	What It Means	How to See It as a Strength
Shortness of breath	The nerves around your rib cage and torso are on high alert, causing you to feel as if some-one is sitting on your chest. In reality, you are breathing just fine and plenty of oxygen is get-ting into your body.	*My body is getting all of the oxygen it needs. This increased breathing rate is going to fuel my muscles and brain with oxygenated blood, so I will be able to think more clearly and react more quickly to what is going on around me.*
Pounding heart	Stress hormones cause your heart rate to speed up so it can pump more blood.	*Plenty of blood is getting to my muscles, fueling me with the energy and strength I need for the job.*
Lump in the throat	The muscles in the throat often constrict when you are anxious.	*Good, I'm a little anxious. Sure this is a little unpleas-ant, but it's not going to kill me. I'd be worried if I didn't feel at least a little anxious. This means I will be on my toes.*
Sweating	The body is preparing itself for battle—for the exertion of fighting or fleeing. Sweating helps cool the body during both.	*Good, my body is ready for this sporting event called life! I don't have to worry about this. If I'm worried what other peo-ple think, I can just joke about how sweaty I am and use it to get a laugh.*

Symptom	What It Means	How to See It as a Strength
Facial tension	The nerves and blood vessels around the face and neck are often the first to become tense when one feels anxious.	*Good—I wanted a sign to help me remember to relax my facial muscles!*
Tingling in the extremities	Blood is surging into your arms and legs to ready you for fight or flight.	*Great—I have so much energy to use to appear more animated. I'll use this energy as I talk with my hands or walk and gesture as I give this speech!*
Dry mouth	Fluids get diverted to the extremities during fight or flight, which can leave your mouth feeling parched.	*Good—this will give me an excuse to take a sip of water. As I sip the water, I will have a chance to collect my thoughts.*

Exercise #5: Create a Fear Response Strategy

You are almost ready to face your fear! But first you need a strategy. It's one thing to know how to turn on your fear response, how to turn it off, and how to use the response to your advantage. It's another to use these strategies in real life. For that, you need a strategic plan. You want to think about exactly how you will deal with your fear response when it arises in specific situations. What will you do? How will you do it? What will be your strategy?

Will you tense and release your muscles? Will you go to your happy place for a second? What will you do and when?

In addition to your relaxation strategy, you'll want to try several other Fear Reducers and incorporate them into your Fear Response Strategy. Write this in your Fearless Notebook. Here are some tips and tricks that clients have used in various situations that tend to bring up their stress response. Pick and choose among them and add a few of your own.

Relax your jaw. Doing so will help to relax your whole body. For instance, when I was worried about how I would appear the first time I went on TV, I relaxed myself by allowing my bottom jaw and lip to pout to loosen up the facial muscles. It works every time!

Stretch. Do it just before going into a stressful situation to relax your muscles.

Pace. It allows you to work some of the energy out of your system.

Talk with your hands. Some people try to be careful about talking with their hands. They worry that doing so will come off as unprofessional. I've found that restricting your movements tends to restrict your thinking and language. It's better to be able to think clearly so you can present your views naturally than it is to hold your arms stiffly at your sides.

Focus on a friendly face in the audience. This will help you to feel more relaxed during speeches and presentations and provides comfort.

Focus on the person you are with and not on yourself. This is especially helpful in the bedroom. For example, forget about your genitals and worry about your partner's genitals instead.

Squeeze and release your butt or another muscle group. No one can see you do it, and it helps to induce the relaxation response.

Focus on relaxing your facial muscles. Your lips, tongue, and eyes are all within your control and sometimes it's easier to zero in on one muscle than your whole body.

Bring your attention to something in the moment. You might, for instance, focus on what someone is saying. This takes your attention off your own fear response. Focus on what someone is saying and his or her mouth and lips as they say it. This provides visual and auditory cues that help you also to remember the information.

See yourself being successful. This is what I do. Before I head into a fearful situation, I visualize myself doing what I fear—and doing it with confidence and calm.

Visualize yourself handling fear with ease. Before you head into a fearful situation, see yourself dealing with a dry mouth or shaky hands ahead of time and being okay with it. This will increase the chance you are okay with it if you are confronted with the fear response in real life. It provides predictability also.

Exercise #6: De-stress Your Life

Many of us are under constant low-level stress. This means that we have stress hormones running through our bodies at all times. Rather than the fear system switching on and then returning to normal, it's always on. This means your muscles are tense, your blood pressure is higher than normal, your heart and breathing rate are faster than normal, and it's easier for your body to get to a completely anxious place. You feel nervous or tense or on edge most of the time. So it takes only a little bit to push you over the edge.

To help get in control of the fear response in specific situations, it will help to keep general stress levels low. If you are calmer and more relaxed all the time, you won't have as difficult a time remaining calm when in the face of fear.

To de-stress your life, pick from among the following strategies, doing as many of them as possible.

- **Exercise.** Work out aerobically three to four times a week and strength-train one to two times a week. This doesn't have to be intense and it doesn't have to be a long work-out. Be creative. Take the stairs at work. Walk during your lunch break. Work movement into your daily routine. Get out there and move.

- **Devote a half day to yourself on your day off from work.** Most people are so busy and their schedules are so full that they are running from one thing to another, and they don't even have time to think about how their bodies feel. They are out of touch with themselves. To counter this, allow at least a half day every week to have no plans whatsoever. Have a block of time where you plan to not plan. You are not knocking items off a to-do list. You are not getting your house as clean as possible. You are just hanging out. Sure you can read or cook or do something that you want to do. But there's no structure and no to-do list.

- **Be good to yourself.** Get regular pedicures or massages or soak weekly (or nightly) in the tub. Watch movies, read, or relax in some other ways. Find regular ways to let go and relax.

- **Manage your time and prioritize tasks.** Realize there's only so much you can do in a given day and that it's counterpro-ductive to spread yourself too thin. Knock off easy tasks on your to-do list first to give yourself a sense of accomplish-ment. Break tasks into what needs to happen today, this week, and this month. Prioritizing ensures success early and motivates you to keep tackling your list.

- **Give yourself chill breaks.** Create five-minute mini-breaks during your day when you do not have stimulation. There's no conversation, no loud sounds, and no visual stimulation.

Feeling Less Tense?

I sure hope you are! You've accomplished a lot with this step of the program. I hope you are already seeing some of the results. Perhaps you are sleeping more soundly or feeling less jumpy than you usually do. Maybe you have even found that you've remained calmer during various life crises than you have in the past. Remember to jot down such changes and benefits in your Fearless Notebook. That way you can read them over to remind yourself of how far you've come.

Fearless Makeover

Cindy came to me because of neck and back pain that always seemed to set in at the end of the workday. She'd gone to several doctors who found nothing structurally wrong with her back or neck. One doctor told her that he thought her symptoms were psychosomatic, which refers to a physical disorder that is brought on or aggravated by emotional factors. He referred her to me.

Cindy was convinced that the doctors had missed something and was ready to try acupuncture next. I didn't dissuade Cindy from trying other treatments, but I did concur that her symptoms were probably psychosomatic. After all, Cindy didn't

continued

have back and neck pain in the morning. She had it only toward the end of the workday. I suspected that something was happening at that time of day that was causing her to mentally and physically tense up and trigger those symptoms. I needed to find out what thoughts were leading to the sore back and neck.

The Goal: Cindy's goal was simple. She wanted to be pain free.

The Payoff: If Cindy could find the source of her pain and overcome it, she would feel better, get more done, and even be happier.

The Program: I asked Cindy to jot down her thoughts for a week. I suggested she might take a minute or two at the top of every hour to do the movie screen exercise from Step 3 (Exercise #1). When we looked at her Fearless Notebook a week later, it was easy to see that as the day progressed, Cindy's thoughts grew increasingly more negative. These were some of her thoughts:

How am I going to get to the school on time to pick up the kids?

My colleagues are going to think I'm slacking again.

Damn, I have to prepare dinner and have no idea what to make.

I learned that Cindy arrived at work earlier than most of her colleagues so she could leave early and be home with the kids after school. Her supervisor was aware of this schedule and approved it, but several of Cindy's colleagues were unaware of it. Because of this, Cindy assumed that her colleagues thought that she was a slacker. "They probably don't realize how early I arrive at work," Cindy said. "They probably think that I never put in a full eight hours."

Cindy had been unaware of all of this thinking. She didn't even know she had these thoughts about her coworkers! They were just playing in the background—in her unconscious mind—much like a subliminal tape.

And these thoughts were leading to anxiety, worry, and frustration. Those feelings were causing her to tense her muscles, causing headaches and neck and back pain that set in during the latter few hours of her workday. Cindy then worked to reframe her negative thinking (Step 3), relax her muscles (Step 4), and even be more assertive with her coworkers (Step 5).

The Outcome: Cindy's neck and back pain subsided and she was able to stop taking painkillers.

Chapter Ten

Step 5: Live Your Dream

In the previous four steps, you overcame the mental obstacles that, until now, have been keeping you stuck and preventing you from taking steps toward your goal. It's my hope that at this point in the plan you are already feeling a sense of freedom, hope, and excitement for opportunities that lie ahead.

In this final step of the program, I'm going to help you overcome some of the physical obstacles that stand between you and your dream. To understand what those physical obstacles are I'd like you to think of two different scenarios.

In Scenario #1, imagine that you get a letter in the mail. It's from NASA. It says, "You have won a chance to go to the moon!" You learn that NASA has randomly picked you out of millions of other Americans as part of a public relations stunt. It's the opportunity of a lifetime. You've always wanted to ride in a rocket ship. Now's your chance! At the end of the letter, however, a bolded sentence catches your eye. It says, "The rocket leaves two weeks from now."

How do you feel? I don't know about you, but if I read a letter like that I would feel scared out of my mind. I doubt I would accept the opportunity. I'd wimp out!

Now, let's imagine Scenario #2. You get the same letter. Only this time, NASA tells you that the space mission is at least a year away. For the next year, NASA promises to train you in space flight. You will go to space school, learn everything there is to know about rocket repair and flight, and ride in various simulators. By flight day you will know what to do, what to expect, and how to handle emergencies that come up.

Now how do you feel? A little anxious, but also a bit excited? Same with me.

I mentioned these two scenarios because most people go through life expecting themselves to be able to deal with Scenario #1. They think they should be able to find the courage, for instance, to feel zero anxiety over giving a toast at a wedding, despite the fact that they've never given a toast or a speech before or taken a class on the topic. Or they think it should be easy for them to start writing a book even though they haven't written anything longer than a book report since twelfth grade. They don't understand why they continually put "writing a book" on their to-do list but never actually write it. Or they don't understand why they get nervous at the prospect of twenty people coming to their home for an elaborate dinner party when they usually cook only simple meals for their own families.

And when they lack the courage to attempt such feats, they beat themselves up and say things like, "I can't believe I'm such a wimp," "I can't believe I had to take a Xanax before I did that," and "I don't understand why I keep procrastinating."

What they don't realize is that *most* people don't have the courage to deal with the Scenario #1s in life. When we see people doing courageous feats, it's usually because those very people are performing feats that are a lot more like Scenario #2—for them, anyway.

For instance, as I've mentioned, my brother is a police officer in Washington, D.C. In June 2004, when Ronald Reagan's body was lying in state at the Capitol, thousands of people—ranging from the general public to dignitaries from around the world—came to pay their final respects to the former president. The week was bustling with activity and heightened security.

In the middle of this week, a plane passed into restricted airspace around D.C. People began to panic. Matthew said, "People were running every which way. They thought the plane was headed right into the White House or the Capitol or another important government building." I asked Matthew if he was anxious. He calmly explained, "No, not at all. I'm trained to keep order and peace in a crisis situation. I've been trained in procedures and know exactly what to do in this type of situation. When I remain calm and collected, it transfers to the people around me."

For all of the panicked people, this was a Scenario #1. They'd never dealt with a plane flying into restricted airspace. The idea of it filled them with uncertainty and fear. *What if it's a terrorist? What am I supposed to do if it's a terrorist? Where will I go if it's a terrorist attack?*

Matthew, on the other hand, knew exactly what to do. While he was probably concerned, he wasn't uncertain. He'd trained for that day. So he wasn't panicked. He was calm. For him, this was a Scenario #2.

Similarly, new parents tell me that it was anxiety provoking the first time they put their newborn in a car seat. That's because they had not practiced this skill before having a newborn. They hadn't taken classes, read books, or even watched YouTube videos on the topic. It was a Scenario #1.

My point is that fear rises up when we attempt to do something that we've never done before, and especially when we attempt to do it without reading or learning about it first. In this final step of the plan, you are going to take what is now a Scenario #1 for you, and you will turn it into a Scenario #2. In this way, you will turn uncertainty into certainty, your fear into the fearlessness, and the impossible into the possible so you can go on and reach your dreams and beyond.

Change Your Life in Two Weeks!

Step 5 includes two exercises. One of them won't take you very long. The other will take time as you put all of your hard work into practice. Depending on the goal you've set for yourself, you may reach it very quickly—as soon as days or weeks from now. If it is a complex dream (such as a career change) it will take longer. Designate a lot of space in your Fearless Notebook for this step.

☐ **Exercise #1:** Create your Fearless Action Plan. Use the sample action plans in the bonus section for guidance. **Estimated time:** 30 to 45 minutes.

☐ **Exercise #2:** Embark on your plan, modifying it over time as needed. **Estimated time:** 2+ weeks.

Exercise #1: Craft Your Fearless Action Plan

Until now, you've probably thought of fearlessness as an elusive mental state—a state that some people have and others don't.

I'd like you to instead think of fearlessness as a muscle, one that becomes weaker with neglect and stronger with exercise.

Your Fearless Action Plan will help you to exercise and strengthen that muscle. This plan isn't much different from a fitness plan. For instance, most runners (the sane ones, anyway) follow a training plan to get in shape for a marathon. They don't wake up one day and say "I'm going to run 26.2 miles" without training for that distance. No, they start out with a distance they can handle and they slowly add miles over time until they are eventually in shape to go the full 26.2. In this way, they slowly and steadily build the strength and endurance they need to go the distance.

You will follow a similar plan that will help you get in shape—mentally and physically—to tackle your ultimate goal and create the life you deserve. This is the culmination of all the work you've done until now. I've come up with several tips that will help you create your plan. In the bonus section at the end of this book, you'll also find several sample Fearless Action Plans you can use for ideas and guidance. Use the tips and sample Fearless Action Plans to create your plan.

Sketch your plan on paper. As I've said, putting it in writing helps hold you accountable, keeps you organized, and helps you to see where important pieces are missing and where there might be unnecessary overlap. Don't plan in your head. Plan on paper—always.

Think small. My very first television experience did not go as well as I'd hoped, and that's because I took too big of a step too soon. I tried to teach myself to perform live as some people used to teach kids to swim. I tossed myself onto the national stage with almost no preparation. It was after that less-than-stellar experience that I realized I needed to take smaller, more realistic steps! That's when I began studying public speaking, communication, and self-presentation, and it's when I began practicing my lines in front of a mirror and other people.

In contrast, think of the story I told you about David. Think of how easily he seemed to progress and face his fear of approaching women. Imagine what might have happened if, during the very first session, I suggested he walk up to the most beautiful woman he saw and ask her out. He would have panicked, right? And that panic would have reinforced his idea that he was no good with women.

Similarly, when my friend Erica wanted to get over her fear of public speaking, she didn't just show up in front of a room of four hundred people and attempt to deliver a speech. No, she started small, with the first step being a passive one: reading about public speaking. Then she practiced in front of a mirror and later in front of her husband. When she did speak, she did so in front of smaller crowds and in environments where she felt comfortable. She also started off with easier presentations, such as Q&A sessions, and advanced her way to more elaborate speeches.

It's the same for you. You want to create several mini-goals that will eventually take you to your ultimate goal. Each small mini-goal should take you just far enough out of your comfort zone that you feel a little excited, but not so far out of your comfort zone that you feel as if you are going to have a panic attack. You might be a little uncomfortable, and that's okay. You shouldn't, however, feel on the edge of panic.

On a 1 to 10 scale—with 1 being "no biggie" and 10 being "I am so panicked that I think I am having a heart attack"—each mini-goal should feel like a 2 or a 3. If a mini-goal is higher than a 6, you don't have enough mini-goals worked into your action plan. You've set the stepping-stones too far apart, and when you attempt to hop from one to the next you will probably fall into the water!

Think about what led to your fear in the first place. Think about past failures and challenges. What can you learn from them? What led to them? What are some mini-actions you can work into your action plan that will help you to overcome those challenges?

Anticipate challenging and tough times. If you are leaving a dead-end relationship, part of your action plan will center on finding ways to overcome your fear of being alone. You might want to anticipate how you will feel during potentially problematic times. When are you likely to want to backpedal? What feelings will lead to emotional weakness for you? What will you do when your anniversary rolls around? What will you do over the holidays? How will you keep yourself busy so that you are not tempted to relapse and call your ex during these tough moments? Come up with a strategy for these problematic times, and plan that strategy into your action plan.

Share your plan with your Fearless Support Team. Talk over each mini-goal. Will each mini-goal serve as a stepping-stone to the next? Are the stones placed the proper distance apart? Should you add additional mini-goals to make your plan more realistic and improve your chances of success?

Set deadlines for each mini-goal. This, again, will help to hold you accountable and keep you from wimping out.

Helpful Tools

Below are a few tools, strategies, and techniques that you may want to incorporate into your action plan.

- **Relaxation training.** You learned relaxation strategies in Step 4. Think about incorporating them into your action plan. For instance, if you have a fear of public speaking, you might practice your relaxation strategy (if possible) in the room where you plan to deliver a speech. You might do this several times until you feel comfortable in that room. Then you might practice again just before you deliver the speech.

- **Visualization.** Before tackling any big goal or even some of your smaller ones, it can help to think about and see yourself doing it. See yourself doing what you fear—and doing it successfully. If you are scared to face your boss about a thorny work issue, imagine the encounter first and see it going well. Also imagine yourself dealing with various challenges with grace, and being okay with them. This will help you to anticipate challenges and plan for them.

- **Role playing.** Practice what you fear in front of a mirror, in an empty room, or with a friend. For instance, if you are having a conflict with a colleague, you might practice what you will say ahead of time.

- **Rewards.** Consider rewarding yourself for small successes that you achieve along the way. This will keep you motivated. It will also help you to see how much progress you've made. It's easy to focus on failures or on what you have yet to achieve, and then get defeated. These rewards will also help you to strengthen the many positive reference experiences you'll be having along the way. Here are some rewards some of my clients have used as they've achieved small victories: a manicure or pedicure, a dinner out, a movie, a great vacation, and time off from work.

- **Research.** Knowledge is one of the best fear antidotes around. For example, a few years ago my dad was diagnosed with prostate cancer. I suggested he and Mom learn everything they could about it. I even suggested a book for them to read together before meeting with the surgeon. They said they found the knowledge helpful and it reduced their stress over the diagnosis.

Exercise #2: Embark on Your
Fearless Action Plan

Once you have the plan on paper, it's time to execute it! As you follow your plan, use this advice:

Be flexible and adjust your goals according to circumstances. It's possible, no matter how carefully you design your Fearless Action Plan, you will fall into the water anyway. For instance, many years ago, I worked with Ed, a man who had social anxiety. I took him to a grocery store and asked him to pick the least-threatening-looking person he could find, then walk up to that person and ask for the time. He decided to walk up to a little old lady. After all, little old ladies are fairly nonthreatening.

Well, Ed was a large guy, about six feet two inches tall and 230 pounds. He was also African-American. What I had not anticipated when I'd asked him to do this exercise was the prejudicial fear some people have of African-American men, especially large men like Ed.

Well Ed asked this little old lady for the time. She turned on her heel and went straight to security and reported to them that Ed was threatening her. The next thing Ed and I knew, a security officer was questioning us. Ed said, "I just asked her for the time." Eventually we worked it out. Ed recovered and went on to overcome his anxiety, but the story shows that at times, your best efforts will sometimes backfire. No action plan is failproof. Be willing to adjust yours as necessary.

If you find yourself procrastinating, work through it. One common cause of procrastination is unrealistic goals that leave you feeling overwhelmed. So go back and check that Fearless Action Plan. Are your stepping-stones too far apart?

Another cause of procrastination is simple hesitation. This is caused by thinking too much and doing too little. After all, it's the thinking time that messes people up and leads to procrastination. You might find that you have to treat this the same way you probably treat jumping into cold water on a warm day. You hold your nose and do a cannonball. Take the plunge. Don't think. Just do!

Finally, it also might help to weigh the stress and disappointment of staying stuck against the overwhelmingly good feeling and satisfaction you will get once you finally take action. Get out that Fearless Notebook again. Draw a line down the middle of a page. On one side of the page list how life will be different one week, one month, and one year from now once you move into action. On the other side, list how life will be one week, one month, and one year from now if you do nothing.

Which result would you rather achieve?

Involve your support team. This is the most critical time to keep them involved! Make them aware of your Fearless Action Plan. Let them know how you are progressing. Tell them when you are about to embark on each step. Just the idea of knowing that your team will be calling you, e-mailing you, and asking you in person about your progress will help you to find the courage to keep moving forward!

Keep a success tally. Remember the negativity bias I mentioned earlier? Don't let it erode your confidence. Whenever you have a setback on your Fearless Action Plan, you may find that you obsess over it and dwell on your failure. That's why it's so important to continually remind yourself of each and every success, because these successes will fuel your confidence. Every time you move forward on your plan, check it off in your Fearless Notebook and jot down a few notes about how the experience was positive for you. Then, if you ever suffer a crisis of confidence, look back over those notes to remind yourself of how far you've come.

Now Get Out There and Live!

Now you know everything you need to know to accomplish that dream. No one is holding you back. Nothing stands in your way. You can do this. You really can! For more inspiration and help, please feel free to visit me at JonathanAlpert.com.

The time has come. The rest of your life is waiting. Get out there and live it.

Fearless Makeover

When he was eighteen, Mike was diagnosed with leukemia and had gone through grueling treatments, which included daily doses of chemotherapy. Initially, his prognosis was grim. At one point Mike's doctor had even said, "I'm not so sure you'll ever leave this hospital." But he didn't die. After months of excruciating treatment, Mike beat the cancer! But now, at age twenty-three, he was living as if he were a fugitive, always looking back over his shoulder. He worried: "Will the cancer return? Will I get sick again? What if the cancer isn't really gone? What if the tests are wrong? What if I have cancer right now and I just don't know it? How much time do I really have? Would it all come to an end?"

As a result, he was taking classes at a junior college, but none that thrilled him. He worked at a restaurant, but he certainly wasn't passionate about the job. He was living at home, and his social and dating life was almost nonexistent. Mike was depressed and aimless. His life was monotonous and routine. He was afraid to get too deeply interested in anything because

continued

he worried that he would lose it. He wasn't really living. He was simply getting by.

The Goal: Mike wanted to live life to the fullest every day. He wanted to do something he was passionate about and look forward to his future with optimism and confidence.

The Payoff: Mike would get his life back, feel in control, and find happiness.

The Program: In session I helped Mike to understand his thoughts and beliefs. Anytime he felt weak, I had him write down his strengths (Step 2). Anytime he thought negatively or had his doubts, I referred him back to the facts of his medical status (Step 3). Whenever he felt lost and aimless, I reminded him of what a remarkable young man he was and the great odds that he had already defied.

I told him that anything was possible, even the impossible. He'd already proven this just by beating the cancer. Mike, after all, was no stranger to defying the odds.

Mike's mood started to improve. He felt strong and was able to reflect on how far he'd come in life in only twenty-three years. Eventually he saw that he had a gift. His story was one of hope and inspiration. Whenever he talked about his remarkable journey, his mood changed dramatically. His eyes opened wide and lit up. I really believed he had a gift.

"You could probably help a lot of people," I told him.

He seemed excited by that prospect. Gone was the listless Mike I'd first encountered. In his place was a passionate young man who wanted to make a difference and who wanted to turn what had once been a limitation into a strength. I challenged him to do just that (Step 5).

The Outcome: Mike is healthy and ambitious. He's done media interviews to help raise awareness and support for cancer patients, and he is thinking big. He's planning to ride his bike from California to New York to help raise money for cancer programs. I recently e-mailed him to ask him how everything was going. This is what he wrote back:

"I've become a fearless, motivated, and passionate advocate for cancer patients. Every single day when I wake, I try to figure out how to translate my success and experience to others around me. During my cycling trip, I intend to stop at various cancer hospitals along my journey, to visit current cancer patients. My intention is to motivate these patients into living for their dreams and doing whatever it takes to survive."

Chapter Eleven

Be Fearless for Life

During my final session with clients, I often review notes from our first session together. This gives them an opportunity to reflect on just how far they've come. My clients are often amazed by how different they are at the end of therapy than they were in the beginning. Frequently they exclaim, "I can't believe I was so stuck," "I can't believe I was so negative back then," and "I never dreamed that this could ever be possible for me."

It's usually during this last discussion that a client will tell me, "You know, I was convinced that I was hopeless. Even when you seemed so confident that you could help me, I thought for sure that I was an exception to the rule. I figured I was going to be the one person who was too messed up for you to help."

This sentiment is actually a lot more common than you would ever suspect. It's a common fear, one that stems from that negativity bias that we've talked about so much throughout the pages of this book.

Perhaps you even felt this way yourself. When you first picked up this book, maybe you doubted yourself. But look at where you are now. Look at how far you've come!

I hope you are now feeling the power of what's possible. You just did something amazing. You reached a dream—one that you didn't think you could ever reach. I hope you feel great about what you've accomplished.

Over the course of this program, you've not only reached an important goal, you've also proved many life-changing lessons to yourself. They are:

- Everyone feels fear. The sensation of fear is no excuse for avoiding what you really want in life.
- You are capable of more than you ever dreamed.
- Nothing is standing between you and the life you really want except for one thing: you.
- Being rejected doesn't make you a reject. Failing at something doesn't make you a failure. Losing doesn't make you a loser. It's better to get rejected, fail, and lose than it is to stay stuck and not try to change your life.
- If you retreat, the fear grows stronger. If you face it, the fear weakens.
- Fear isn't a reason to stop, stay stuck, or avoid what you want. It's a sign to go for it!
- You are bigger and stronger than your fear.
- You can control your fear response, and you can turn it into a strength.
- What you once thought was impossible is really possible.

How does it feel to be fearless? I hope you feel on top of the world right now. Take a moment to relish this sense of accomplishment.

But don't stop here.

You may have initially picked up this book because you were interested in overcoming a specific fear-related issue. Maybe you wanted to get past a fear of public speaking or a fear of rejection. And you did it. That's fantastic!

But keep going. Now that you've crossed one goal off your Dream List, it's time to find another goal to work on. Remember: fearlessness is like a muscle. The more you use the muscle, the stronger it gets. The less you use it, the weaker it gets. If you stop here, you'll regress. Rather than continually growing in your fearlessness, you'll eventually backslide and end up where you started. Sure, you might not lose the goal you initially achieved, but you will probably find yourself feeling incapacitated with fear over something else.

I don't want that to happen to you! I don't want you to regress into the old you. No, I want you to be like Lisa, one of many of my clients who went from fearful to fearless. What follows is her amazing story of transformation.

Lisa's Quest for Fearlessness

On a Sunday afternoon in August 2011, I received a call. It was Lisa. She was ecstatic and was crying tears of joy. She was so excited that she had trouble getting words out.

"I did it! I did it! I did it!" she said breathlessly. She didn't have to say anymore. I knew what she had done. She'd just completed the New York City Triathlon. She'd swam 1,500 meters in the Hudson River, biked 40 kilometers around New York City, and run a 10K. She had every reason in the world to be ecstatic and proud.

She was on top of the world and now felt nearly invincible. Yet, just six months before, Lisa had been a mess.

Back in February, when Lisa first came to me, her marriage of seven years was in trouble. Her sex life was nonexistent. She felt unfulfilled in her job as an administrative assistant. She regularly had conflicts with her spouse and her coworkers. She thought her two kids, aged two and four, were out of control. She was out of shape, and she had no idea what her future held. She was depressed and anxious. She regularly self-medicated with junk food. Her health was poor and her stress levels were high. She was miserable.

Simply put, she was fearful and destined to become even worse.

At session one I asked Lisa what was most important to her. She told me that she didn't know. This did not surprise me. Lisa, at that time, was entirely focused on what she thought was wrong with her life: her marriage, her career, her health, her kids. She couldn't begin to envision what a good life might look and feel like. So I gave her some homework that was essentially Step 1 of the BE FEARLESS program. I asked her to think about how she would want her life to be if she didn't feel stuck and weighed down by all of her so-called problems. "What would you be doing?" I asked. "What would your life be like if you were happy?" I wanted Lisa to mentally disconnect from what she saw as daunting and insurmountable and to get out of her victim mentality. I wanted her to start thinking about what was possible. I wanted her to dream.

Lisa came back the next week and had completed her homework, but she made something very clear. "I did it, but only because you asked me to and I know I'll never be able to actually do these things," she said.

Her list was compelling. She wanted to improve communication with her husband and ultimately improve her marriage. She also wanted to get in shape and have a job she loved.

I pushed her. "Specifically what can *you* do to be a better communicator at home? What can *you* do to get in shape? And what's *your* dream job?"

The following week she came in with answers. "I always

dreamed of running a marathon or doing a triathlon. And for my marriage I want to be a good listener, I want to be patient. I want to feel good."

Lisa was devoted. She was working hard. I knew she'd be a success and I told her so. In the weeks that followed I taught her how to better communicate with her husband. I taught her how to take care of her needs so she no longer became resentful and angry toward him. We were gaining some traction, some momentum. I knew Lisa needed something huge to work toward. She needed a goal. The more we talked, the more I learned about her deep passion for health and fitness. She explained that she'd always secretly dreamed of opening a health food store.

"But I could never do that, of course," she said.

I knew different. I knew she could. But I had to prove it to her.

Starting a store was going to be a huge task, but not an impossible one. I also knew that she needed to get in shape if she was going to promote health food.

I knew she needed a goal such as a race or an event, something that would inspire her to believe that anything was possible. I had her choose something. There it was: the New York City Triathlon, August 7, 2011. I marked my calendar and she marked hers. She had six months to prepare. I knew this was no easy task either. We devised a plan. It included her joining a class that met three times a week to train. It also included her talking to her husband to gain his full support. Further, she needed to manage her schedule to make time for the training.

Lisa was disciplined. She got up several mornings a week at 5 a.m. to run, bike, or go to the gym. She got the kids ready for their day, and got herself off to work too by 9 a.m. She was entirely focused and devoted. She was nervous, but also excited. She was results oriented. She was fearless!

At a time in her life when just about everything was a mess, she dug deep within herself, not only to overcome her problems but also to persevere physically and emotionally. She tapped into strength she never knew she had: her ability to define her dream, strategize, and put it all into action and persevere. The triathlon gave her a purpose, a sense of accomplishment, and confidence. This was remarkable, and likely not too different from your own journey.

How to Be Even More Fearless

Lisa is still facing her fears to this very day, and she's doing it without my help. She has grown from a fearful person into a fearless one. She exemplifies what I'd like you to achieve for yourself.

Like Lisa, I want you to keep exercising your fearless muscle. You just crossed one goal off your list. Now it's time to pick another one, and then another one, and then another one. Keep formulating and reaching goals until doing so becomes habitual for you. Eventually, instead of thinking *But I could never do that,* you'll automatically think, *Of course I can do that. I can do anything. I've proven that much to myself.*

Use the following pointers.

Do: Go back to the Dream List from Step 1. Pick another goal off the list and go for it! Progress through the five-step program over and over again, crossing more and more goals off the list.

Do: Add new goals to your Dream List over time. As you grow in your fearlessness, you will find that you will come up with more goals for yourself. In the beginning of your fearless journey, you might have discounted certain goals because you thought that they just weren't possible for you. The more you cycle through the five-step program, the more you will realize that nothing is beyond your reach.

Do: Join me at JonathanAlpert.com and at Facebook.com /JonathanAlpert. Here you will find support, tips, and a community of people who are all trying to do what you are trying to do: Be Fearless.

Do: Help others to be fearless. Teaching the techniques to others helps to strengthen them in your own mind.

Do: Maintain a positive attitude.

Do: Continue to think about why you can, should, and will achieve any goal.

Do: Shift from setting goals based on what you **don't** want to goals based on what you **do** want. Keep in mind what I told you about the difference between inspiration and desperation. Desperation might get you started, but inspiration is more likely to take you the entire distance.

It's okay if your initial goal was about something you don't want in your life, such as a dead-end relationship, an unfulfilling job, or an anxiety problem. Now that you've achieved this initial goal and have built some confidence, it's time for your mind-set to change. This is an important shift in thinking because it's a lot more fulfilling to move toward a positive than it is to move away from a negative. Ultimately you have a choice. You can do things out of inspiration or desperation. But when you do them out of inspiration, your results are stronger and more lasting. Your goals will seem easier to achieve too. And you will gain a greater sense of accomplishment.

Don't: Get overconfident and assume you can just wing it and do it in your head. You might be able to do that eventually. Right now, however, you're still a novice at facing your fear. Use the book and cycle through the five steps until being fearless starts to come naturally to you. You will know when that day comes because you will act fearlessly first—without thinking about it.

Don't: Crumble under peer pressure. Being different might mean that you become unpopular, especially among the people

in your life who are used to the current you. Yet doing things to
fit in will just result in more of the same, and you know where
more of the same has led you: to this book. You want change in
your life; otherwise you would not have picked up this book and
started reading it. Yes, having the courage to be different might
be anxiety provoking, but it's not deadly. Trust me: I have not died
or even been injured from being unique. You won't either.

Don't: Beat yourself up over time wasted. So what if you spent
twenty, thirty, or more years living in fear? I always like to say that
it can take three decades to get your act together. Think about it.
For the first eighteen years you go to school and then you might
go to college for many years. Then you try out different jobs, and
before you know it you might be thirty and settled in a career and
finally starting to live your life.

More important, you've faced your fear and are now fearless.
Stop living in the past. Embrace the present. Push forward.

Don't: Settle for mediocrity. If life doesn't feel good enough, it
probably isn't. Push for more even if you think you can't or might
not have to.

Your Ultimate Life Is Waiting

As my clients are nearing the end of their time with me, I like to
tell them this old story about a huge cruiser that breaks down in
the middle of the sea. Here the cruiser is sitting powerless in the
ocean. There's mass panic as everyone on board contemplates
the worst.

The captain and his crew try everything to get the boat's engine
running again. Nothing works. They become so desperate that
they ask random passengers if any of them knows how to fix a
boat engine.

Thankfully one of them does. This passenger, a young engineer, looks at the engine. Then he picks up a small hammer and taps the engine. Miraculously the engine starts running again! Everyone rejoices and thanks the man.

The engineer hands the boat captain his bill. The captain is stunned.

"Ten thousand dollars? All you did was tap the engine with a hammer!"

The engineer says, "I can itemize it for you if you'd like."

The captain says he would like that very much.

The engineer then hands the captain an itemized bill. It says, "$1 for tapping the engine. $9,999 for knowing where to tap."

I share this story with you for an important reason. Before you read this book, you were like the boat captain. You knew your engine was stuck, but you didn't know how to fix it. Now, however, you are like the engineer. You now have specialized knowledge that few other people have. This knowledge is powerful. It was the knowledge that allowed that engineer to move this huge vessel. It's knowledge that will allow you to do the same.

Now you know where to tap. No matter what causes you to feel stuck, you know exactly how to get unstuck again. You know how to keep your fearless engine running.

This knowledge is powerful. It allows you to make the impossible possible.

Live Every Moment

I'll end this book with some thoughts about the fleeting nature of life and how precious it all is.

For a moment, think about the age of the universe. It's been around for billions of years. Then think of the millions of years it took to create what we now know of as our planet. Just the Rocky Mountains in the Western United States, for instance, have been around for 80 million years! This amount of time is incomprehensible for most.

Now think about the number of years an average human being lives. It might be eighty years or ninety, or even one hundred if that person is lucky. It's a long time, but when you compare it to how long it took to create the earth, mountains, and rivers, it's just a blink. But what a blink it is!

It goes fast. Don't waste it. Make the most of the time you have here. Don't hold back. Forge ahead. Be yourself.

BE FEARLESS! Dream big. Make the impossible possible. Live every moment as if it's your last.

BE
FEARLESS
Essentials

In this part of the book, you'll find many Fearless Action Plans that I've created for my clients over the years. Use them for ideas and inspiration as you create your own. You'll also find several bonus exercises and tips that you can use to overcome various challenges that might arise as you go through the program.

Sample Action Plans

▼

The Goal: **A woman dreams of meeting a guy who is sensitive, funny, doesn't cheat, and isn't afraid of commitment. She's worried that this is impossible because she suspects that all guys are jerks.**

The Plan: Keep your negativity bias in check. Just because you may have dated a few guys who turned out to be jerks doesn't mean all guys are jerks. Know that the longer as you continue to believe they are, the longer you won't find a good guy who meets the criteria of what you *do* want. Accept the notion that there are more loyal and good-hearted people looking for a relationship than there are jerks looking for relationships. Mathematically the odds are in your favor.

1. Actively look for and remind yourself of examples of men who disprove your negativity bias. They don't have to be men you want to date. They could even be family members.

2. Know what your goals, beliefs, and values are in respect to relationships. Make a list of what you are looking for. What qualities are important to you? Think about where you see yourself a year from now, two years from now, and five years from now. Write down what you see.

3. List the qualities this man would ideally possess. What would his personality be like?

4. Know where to look. You could search for dates in bars, but many of the people there might not be looking for a relationship anyway. They might be there just to watch the game or hang out with their friends and not to actually meet someone. Online dating is targeted, while speed dating is efficient. Also consider getting involved in activities that you naturally enjoy. This will ensure that you meet like-minded people. It also eliminates anxiety that often comes with a more formal dating scenario or dating service.

5. Start meeting potential candidates. When dating, look for guys who meet your list of qualities. Think of yourself as an employer who is looking for the right employee for the job.

The Goal: A mother dreams of having more time to herself. She thinks it's impossible because of her two jobs and kids.

The Plan:

1. Think what's possible, not what's impossible.

2. Write a list of your responsibilities—those that you have on a daily basis, weekly basis, and monthly basis.

3. Examine that list. Do you need to actually do everything on the list? Or might you be able to consolidate or reduce the responsibilities?

4. Write a list of how you currently spend your time.

5. Are there times when you can multitask? For example, can you catch up on reading, do paperwork, or pay bills when you might be waiting for your child somewhere?

6. Provide activities for your kids that allow them to be independent, thus freeing up time for you.

7. Depending on the age of your kids, enlist their help. Yours truly was ironing pillowcases and emptying garbage buckets at an early age. This, in part, was how Mom and Dad taught me about being responsible. Simple tasks such as emptying garbage, vacuuming, or dusting not only lighten your workload, but also will provide a sense of responsibility to your kids.

8. Be open to enlisting the help of your significant other.

9. Coordinate schedules with a friend or neighbor to free up some of your time by sharing babysitting and driving duties.

The Goal: **A man wants to give a great toast at his best friend's wedding while seeming confident and perhaps even funny.**

The Plan:

1. Be okay with lowering your expectations of yourself. You're not a professional speaker, and no one expects you to deliver a dazzling impromptu speech. You're first and foremost a friend. Keep in mind that toasts that come from the heart are going to be the most moving and memorable.

2. Write your toast ahead of time. Writing allows you to organize your thoughts by providing a beginning, a middle, and an end. For ideas, think of a toast you've heard that resonated with you. What did you like about it? Was it funny? Was it moving? Keep these elements in mind as you write yours. Also think about what you find to be special about the bride and groom. What do you like about them? Share something unique about them (that's acceptable, of course).

3. Edit your material. Read your toast out loud and time yourself as you do it. Attention spans are short, so the toast should be too. Limit what you prepare to two to three minutes' worth of material.

4. Visualize yourself giving the toast. Imagine the audience and see yourself delivering it with confidence.

5. Practice it ahead of time. You can do this alone, in front of a mirror, or with a friend or two.

6. At the wedding, introduce yourself to the other guests and explain how you know the bride and groom. Speak to the couple and maintain eye contact. Use gestures to emphasize a point. Utilize pauses as well to stress a point and catch your breath. Be warm, keep it simple, and don't feel you have to be a stand-up comedian. It's a happy occasion, so remember to smile! Remember to raise your glass and ask everyone to join you in toasting the couple (Mr. and Mrs. X) and say cheers!

The Goal: A groom wants to dance with his bride even though he is terrified of dancing.

The Plan:

1. Change your thinking. Contrary to what you might think, all eyes are not on you. People tend to watch the person who is lighting up the dance floor more so than the person who is just mediocre or not very good at dancing. They also tend to pay much more attention to the bride than they do to the groom.

2. Examine your expectations. Are they realistic? Do you expect to be like Patrick Swayze in *Dirty Dancing*? Is it more realistic to expect to be like an average person who isn't an actor or a professional dancer?

3. Watch other dancers either in real life, on television, or even online. Notice how they all do it a little differently. Also notice that dancing is about feeling the rhythm and moving to it. That's it. There's no right or wrong way to do it. The way you interpret music might be different from the next person. Be okay putting your unique spin on it.

4. Practice, practice, practice. Take a class and find comfort with people who are also beginners. Practice at home, perhaps with a friend or a mirror. You might even consider practicing with the help of any number of dancing-themed video games.

5. Dance with your bride in a few small, intimate settings before the wedding.

6. While at the wedding, feel inspired by the good dancers rather than intimidated. Copy their moves if appropriate.

The Goal: A woman wants to land her dream job despite economic hard times.

The Plan:

1. Define your dream job. Be specific. For example, what would it entail? Would you be working independently or as part of a team? Would you travel or be office-bound? Do you want something that's analytical or creative? You get the idea. Really define all aspects of this dream job and the qualities you seek in it.

2. Surround yourself with people who can help you achieve your dream job. These should be people who inspire, support, and encourage you. Find someone who can offer guidance and mentor you.

3. Don't reinvent the wheel. Ask other people how they got to where they are. Although your path won't be entirely the same, you might gain some valuable advice from knowing how others have done it.

4. Interview someone who has this dream job. Find out what the person did to land the job. Ask questions that will yield valuable information. Ask not only what they love about their job and what they do on a day-to-day basis, but also what they find most challenging, what they'd most like to change about it, and any regrets they might have.

5. Network, network, network. Each person you meet in the industry can potentially bring you closer to your dream job.

6. Do an internship, or shadow someone at a company that you admire.

7. Apply! Even if a company doesn't list openings, inquire about where and how they might use your skills.

The Goal: A woman wants to be herself in social settings instead of just blending in with others.

The Plan:

1. Before you can be yourself you must know who you are. Think about and write out your convictions, beliefs, passions, values, and strengths. Know what you stand for and what makes you tick. Know where you come from and where you're going.

2. Understand the role that hiding behind a mask plays in your life. Are you shy, anxious, or unsure? Do you feel inadequate or are you afraid to shine?

3. Practice expressing yourself by writing out your thoughts and feelings in your Fearless Notebook. Include how you feel about yourself, situations you might experience on a daily basis, and people you might encounter during the day.

4. Learn to express yourself clearly by practicing with people you trust.

5. Don't care so much about how other people perceive you. The more you do, the more you are trying to fulfill their expectations and the less you will fulfill your own.

6. Do away with social comparison. This only leads to resentment and moves you away from being who you truly are.

The Goal: A mother wants to overcome her fear of going back to school.

The Plan:

1. Know what the fear is about. Is it about the unknown? Failure? Success? Or maybe it's about change and how you'll adjust to adding the school to your schedule.

2. Whatever the fear, address it. Change is stressful, even good change such as going back to school. The best antidote against fear is to become familiar with the stressor. Research the school and program, and understand what it will entail. By doing so you'll become more certain and more familiar with the unknown.

3. Shift your thinking. Rather than focusing on the perceived negatives and challenges that lie ahead, think about what you will gain from going back to school (a degree, job opportunities, social and professional contacts).

4. Meet with the school. Most departments have open houses for prospective students. See this as an opportunity to learn about the program and meet with like-minded people.

5. Ask to audit a class. This will give you a real opportunity to get an idea of what the classes will be like.

6. Get your Fearless Team to support you!

| The Goal: | **A man wants to overcome his fear of asking for a raise** |

| The Plan: |

1. Make a clear and compelling list of how you've made or saved your company money. Write your strengths and why you are an asset to the company.

2. Research the standard salary for your title.

3. Anticipate resistance from your boss and know how to respond. Remember, there are two opposing goals: yours is to make money while his or hers is to save money.

4. Consider negotiating for something other than a salary increase. For instance you might ask for a bonus, extra vacation time, or tuition reimbursement.

5. Visualize the conversation ahead of time. Think of how your boss might respond and what you might say.

6. Practice with a trusted friend.

7. Then go do it. If all else fails, be prepared to ask how you can earn a raise.

| The Goal: | **A woman wants to overcome her fear of buying a new car.** |

| The Plan: |

1. Educate yourself on cars and know what you want and need in a new one.

2. Know your budget and stick to it.

3. See your trip to the showroom as an opportunity to get your best price.

4. Be aware that the salesperson will appeal to your emotions by suggesting things such as "SUVs are safer than cars" or "You'll look great in a convertible with leather seats."

5. Research what the dealer pays for the car as compared to the sale price.

6. Let the salesperson suggest the price first.

7. Remember, you're under no obligation to buy, even if you've taken the car out for a few hours.

8. Be prepared to walk away guilt free.

9. Sleep on any decision to buy or not and reevaluate in the morning.

| The Goal: | **A man wants to overcome his fear of being unemployed forever.** |

| The Plan: |

1. Avoid late nights and sleeping in.

2. Set your alarm and be ready to start your day by 9 a.m. This allows you to mirror that of the mainstream business world and stay connected.

3. Be a go-getter. Your new job is that of a marketing executive, and you are the product.

4. Take an inventory of your strengths and list them on paper. Make sure they are reflected in an updated résumé and cover letter.

5. Compile a list of ten or more contacts, then compose an e-mail to send to them and attach your résumé. Ask them to keep you in mind for any jobs they might know of and also for them to pass your information on to their contacts.

6. Schedule your day. For instance, from 9 a.m. to 10 a.m., answer e-mails. From 10 a.m. to 11 a.m., look at job sites. From 11 a.m. to noon, send out résumés. From noon to 1 p.m., have lunch. You get the idea.

7. Consider volunteering and remember to relax.

The Goal: A woman wants her spouse to help out around the house.

The Plan:

1. Don't boss him, but rather be polite and courteous and treat him the way you'd want to be treated.

2. Empower him by asking him which chores he is most comfortable doing around the house.

3. Define clean. Do you share the same definition as your significant other? Are your expectations reasonable?

4. Compliment him once he starts doing chores. Positive reinforcement will encourage more of the same behavior.

5. Tell him how sexy you find his doing housework. Housework and sex will then be linked in his mind, and that can only help.

The Goal: A man wants to overcome his fear of approaching women.

The Plan:

1. From this point forward, think about any situation that involves approaching someone as an opportunity—an opportunity to meet someone you feel excited about. Any tinge of anxiety is merely your body's response to the opportunity. Remember, the only difference between anxiety and excitement is made in your head and how you interpret physiological signals.

2. Go to a public place, such as a grocery store, a busy park, or a city street. Observe people and relax.

3. Lower your expectations and forget about meeting the next love of your life or even potential date.

4. Smile at people whom you never would want to date, especially people you're not physically attracted to or who might be out of your desired age demographic. Notice how they respond. Smiles usually beget smiles. It's a natural instinct to return one.

5. Progress to a simple "Hello" or asking for the time or directions. There are no expectations or pressure.

6. Grab a park bench and move that hello to something more. Try "It's a beautiful day out here" or another line. Say something that may or may not require a response. This is about you gaining comfort with small talk. Don't worry about what the other person may or may not say back.

7. Now, engage in conversation. Ask open-ended questions such as, "How do you like the park?"

8. Next, choose a setting that provides opportunities to meet people. No, not a bar, but rather a place such as a bookstore. Think about it: a bookstore provides an opportunity to talk about every topic under the sun from travel, business, cooking, sports, politics, religion, self-help, and much more. Potentially there's a conversation waiting to happen on a range of topics. Another possibility is to do something you enjoy. So if you are into running, join a running club. If you are into cooking, take a class.

| The Goal: | **A woman wants to overcome the fear of moving in with her partner.** |

| The Plan: |

1. Write out your motivation. Is it to save money and out of convenience, or is it love and the next step toward marriage?

2. Know that the dynamic in your relationship will likely change when you're living under the same roof.

3. Decide with your partner what you keep and what you get rid of. Holding on to duplicate items will create clutter, which could potentially lead to stress. It also sends a message that the move is temporary.

4. Search for a new place together rather than moving into either of your existing places. The latter could lead to territorial issues down the road.

5. Discuss expectations.

6. Decide before the move how you handle household chores and tasks. Come up with a plan.

7. Agree on a financial plan ahead of time. How will rent, utilities, food, and other expenses be handled? Either split all expenses down the middle or, in the interest of equality, contribute a proportionate percentage of your respective salaries.

Bonus Exercises and Tips

▼

Certain fears and problems crop up over and over again in my clients. I see these same fears in greater society too. What follows are some specific advice, tips, and exercises to help you with these very common issues.

Advice for People Who Fear Commitment:

▶ **Accept what you can't control.** Remind yourself that as long as there are relationships, there will be those that work and those that don't. Control what's in your control: what you do to make your relationship strong.

▶ **Define what a healthy relationship means to you.** If you wanted to open a coffee shop, would you model it after the one that was about to go out of business or the one that was thriving? Rather than focusing on botched relationships, look at relationships that work.

▶ **If you are getting married, enter the marriage 100 percent committed and without divorce as an option.** In relationships that stand the test of time, couples are entirely focused on maintaining their relationships and doing what's necessary to make them work.

▶ **Know that disagreements are normal.** They are not signs of the end. Look at the big picture and ask yourself, *Is it worth it to win the battle but lose the war?* Accept that there will always be certain traits about your partner that may never change. Sure, it may annoy you that she burns the toast—but in the end, does it really matter?

▶ **Focus on what binds you, not on what separates you.** You originally got together because of commonalities, not differences.

▶ **Take time out when there are arguments or fights.** Rarely are issues resolved in the heat of battle, so walk away and agree to come together when things calm down. Examine your intent. Is it to hurt the other person or to work toward a compromise? Avoid absolute words such as *always* or *never*, as they seldom lead to a constructive conversation.

Advice for People
Who Fear Change:

▶ **Accept that every long-term benefit comes with a cost.** It's short-term stress. The good thing about this kind of stress is that it doesn't last forever. It will eventually go away.

▶ **Keep the long-term payoff in mind.** Whenever the stress of change becomes too uncomfortable, remind yourself of those long-term payoffs. Read and reread your Payoff List.

▶ **Once a day visualize yourself doing what you want.** Use this image to outthink your fear of change.

Advice for Dealing
with the Sunday Night Blues:

▶ **Take a step back and look at the big picture.** What makes you anxious about returning to work? Is it based on reality or on something you imagine?

▶ **Decipher fact from fiction.** Focus on what's within your control, not what lies beyond it.

▶ **Prepare for Monday every Friday.** At the end of each workweek, prepare for the next by straightening up your workspace, tying up loose ends, and making a to-do list.

▶ **Relax as much as you can.** When planning your weekend, don't overschedule and certainly don't leave stressful activities for Sunday.

▶ **Plan your Sunday according to your mood.** If you ordinarily feel depressed on Sundays, then plan a fun activity such as a special dinner out or hanging out with friends. If you typically find yourself edgy, then indulge in something relaxing such as a movie or reading.

▶ **Balance your sleep patterns.** If you get up at 6 a.m. during the week but sleep in on the weekends, you may not be tired come bedtime on Sunday. Leave Saturday for sleeping in. On Sunday try not to deviate too far from your regular wake-up time.

▶ **Stop staring at the clock.** Turn your alarm clock away from the bed so that you aren't reminded of your approaching workday. Have confidence that it will wake you at the appropriate time.

▶ **Count your blessings.** Before you go to sleep, identify three positive things about your job or the day ahead. Drift off to sleep looking forward to what you like about your job rather than dreading what you don't like.

Advice for
Perfectionists:

▶ **Make a few small mistakes on purpose.** Be messy. Leave a typo. See that you can make a mistake and not contribute to the end of the world.

▶ **Look at the positive traits of something and at the facts.** Don't focus only on the negative aspects or the perceived shortcomings.

▶ **Set reasonable goals.** They should be flexible and change over time.

▶ **Kill that dichotomous thinking.** Accept that there are more options than perfect and worthless. Aim for somewhere in the middle.

Advice for
<u>Seniors Who Fear Retirement</u>:

▶ **Pinpoint the underlying fear.** Think about where it comes from. Is it about making ends meet without a steady income? Is it about what you'll do with your abundance of free time? Is it about how you'll get along with your spouse now that you'll be seeing more of each other? How do you envision retirement? What are your expectations? Have a plan or an idea of what you'd like it to be like.

▶ **If you have a spouse, then discuss it with him or her and be open to compromise.** Recognize that any differences you might have are okay and can be worked out. Accept the notion that time apart is okay. You've spent time apart for years in your respective careers, so you've proven that you can make it.

▶ **Reduce financial uncertainty.** Meet with a financial planner to discuss how to manage finances, expenses, and investments.

▶ **Stay active, both physically and mentally.** This will help keep you healthy and provide structure to your day.

▶ **Remember, you don't lose the skills, expertise, and experience you've amassed over your career.** There's a place for them. Perhaps it is in mentoring or simply providing support to someone.

▶ **Volunteer and get involved.** This will fill the void that results from your retiring by creating a sense of belongingness.

Advice for People
Whose Work Keeps Them Up at Night:

▶ **Focus on the things you have control over, not on what's beyond it.** Focus your thoughts on what you can do rather than on what you can't.

▶ **Every day when you get home from work, make a to-do list for the next day.** Put it with your bag by your door. Leave it there.

▶ **Shut off all electronic devices related to work at least an hour before bedtime.** Do something relaxing instead such as reading or watching TV. Or try Progressive Muscle Relaxation or another relaxation technique.

▶ **Think of three things from your day you feel good about.** It doesn't matter how minor you think they are. It might be a good conversation you had with a friend or a tasty lunch. Then think about three things you look forward to the next day.

Advice for
Overcoming the Fear of Airport Security:

▶ **Understand that security employees are doing their job.** You both share a common goal: to get you from point A to point B as safely and efficiently as possible.

▶ **Don't let the airport define your trip.** It's simply a mode of transportation. Don't personalize any security efforts or measures.

▶ **Do your part to ensure a smooth transition through security.** Actually do all the things they ask: have your boarding pass and identification ready, dress simple, don't wear any extraneous metal, lose the belt and shoes, and know which items are acceptable and unacceptable to bring on board.

▶ **Allow extra time in your schedule and anticipate delays.** Know that boredom breeds agitation, so bring something to occupy your time such as a book, music, or video games.

Advice for People
Who Fear Terrorism:

▶ **Accept the notion that uncertainty is part of the fabric of our society.** We will never know what terrorists are thinking or where they might strike next. Focus on what you know rather than on what you don't.

▶ **Separate fact from fiction.** Write two columns on a piece of paper. On one side write what you know to be fact and on the other write what might be more rumor and hype. Put an X through the second column and focus only on the facts.

▶ **Choose a news source that you trust and stick with it.** Stay away from news sources that indulge in fearmongering.

▶ **Decide on a news exposure budget.** Decide how much news you'll expose yourself to and allot a limited time to watching the news. For instance, it might be just in the morning and evening. Know that if anything major happens you'll find out in due time.

▶ **Maintain structure and routine in your day.** Remember, anxiety in part stems from uncertainty, so do your part to make your day predictable.

▶ **Feelings of helplessness feed fear, so be proactive.** Volunteering or sending goodies overseas to soldiers are two ways you can take charge and help someone in need.

Advice for
**Pregnant Women
Who Fear Motherhood:**

▶ **Talk to friends and family who have kids to learn how they do it.** Ask all of the questions that are on your mind, even those that you are afraid to ask. For instance, ask, "Do you ever feel you could undo it?" and "Do you ever wish you could give the baby back?"

▶ **Do research to find out the actual cost of raising a child and then work out a practical plan with your partner to handle the added expenses.** If you come up short, then explore support from friends and family and look into money-saving cuts in your current lifestyle.

▶ **Separate normal mommy-to-be jitters from those that might be irrational.** Examine the irrational ones and search for any supporting evidence. If none are found, explore alternative ways of viewing the situation. For example, "I'll never be able to travel once I have a child" might be replaced by "Travel is more challenging, but there are kid-friendly destinations I can look into and enjoy."

▶ **Share your concerns with your partner, as he might be feeling the same.** Most first-time parents feel at least some anxiety, and even doubt. Tap your partner for support.

Advice for People
in Long-Distance Relationships:

▶ **Define the relationship and have an end goal.** Are you exclusive to each other or just dating? Have a conversation with your significant other about your respective needs, what you both want out of the relationship, and what you're currently getting out of it.

▶ **Schedule times to speak.** Maintain daily contact to ensure a strong emotional connection. Be imaginative, creative, and sexy, and utilize Skype and webcam technology. Whenever possible rely on direct communication, and avoid instant messaging and texting. There's too much opportunity for misinterpretation using these methods.

▶ **Schedule visits too.** This gives you something to look forward to and puts parameters around the long-distance relationship. Knowing that you'll see each other certain weekends and holidays should provide comfort. Plan vacations together to create newness and progression in the relationship rather than just maintaining the status quo.

▶ **Replicate doing things together as best as possible.** For example, watch a television show or movie simultaneously and talk about it after.

Advice for
<u>City Dwellers with Sidewalk Rage</u>:

▶ **Change your thinking.** You have an idea of how you think others *should* be: keep to the right, walk at a certain pace, keep moving. In a perfect world people would follow such etiquette. But there are no universal rules. People can walk as they wish. Accept this notion.

▶ **Keep things in perspective.** Know that the difference between a healthy pedestrian and a rager is the latter has a negative view of others, is overly sensitive, overgeneralizes, and blows things out of proportion. The rager might think, *I'm going to be so late* or *This sucks.* Angry venting only reinforces the thoughts and makes them occur more automatically.

▶ **Don't personalize things.** Rather than thinking, *What an idiot this person is for walking so slowly,* look at alternative explanations. Is it possible that he might be lost or simply not see you?

▶ **See the whole sidewalk.** Walk tall and look straight ahead to get a full view of all angles ahead of you.

▶ **Stay away from crowds, if possible.** Keep in mind, the greater the population, the slower the pace. Use a less traveled alternative route.

▶ **Have some empathy.** Remember, the people you're cursing could be someone's loved one. Think how you would want your loved ones to be treated in a similar situation.

Advice for
Smokers Who Want to Quit:

▶ **Forget the programs that guarantee results in two days.** There's no magical pill or workshop that will lead to instantaneous and lasting results. Breaking an addiction requires dedication, commitment, and hard work—the same ingredients you need to achieve any goal.

▶ **Deal with the short-term stress.** Accept that immediately after quitting, hunger may increase and you may snack a little more. Your metabolism (which increases during smoking) will also be restored to a normal rate. This is part of the process of quitting, but it's temporary.

▶ **Remind yourself of the choice you made.** In order to reap the long-term benefits of better health, you've made the choice to endure the temporary stress and discomfort of withdrawal symptoms.

▶ **Make a Payoff List.** On it list all of the reasons you want to stop smoking, such as better health, saving money, and fresher breath. Review your Payoff List daily.

▶ **Set a quit date.** Put it on the calendar and enlist friends and family for support and motivation.

▶ **Line up a sponsor.** Find someone who can keep you accountable and give you a kick in the butt when necessary.

▶ **Get rid of all cigarettes, matches, lighters, and ashtrays.** You're quitting so you don't need them. And keeping them around will only give you visual triggers that cause you to think about smoking.

▶ **Understand that the first two to three weeks will be the toughest.** That's when your psychological withdrawal symptoms will be strongest. Remind yourself that this tough time is temporary. You can get through it. During this time indulge in lollipops, gum, carrots, or celery sticks to keep your mouth occupied and satisfy your oral fixation.

▶ **Anticipate tough times.** Stressful situations may increase the likelihood of relapse, so anticipate them and come up with a plan to manage your stress. For instance, tap into support or take up a new hobby that distracts you from thinking about smoking.

▶ **Form new habits.** Replace what was once your smoke break with a new activity such as a brisk walk or healthy snack. If you paired smoking with drinking, limit the alcohol and eat nuts instead of smoking. If you used to smoke following a meal, do something else to replace that habit. For instance, get up, wash dishes, and brush your teeth.

▶ **Place notes in key places around your house and office to remind yourself of your goal.** They might say something like, "I'm a non-smoker, and feel healthy, clean, and strong."

▶ **Put the money you normally would spend on cigarettes in a jar or bank.** Use it to reward yourself for the progress you've made. Movies, dinners, and nights on the town will motivate you to enjoy your new smoke-free life.

Advice for
Social Media Addicts:

▶ **Know the difference between an online and a real-life friend.**
Make a list of the benefits and drawbacks of each.

▶ **Ask yourself the true reason for being online.** If it's to engage
in social interaction, then make direct contact or use the telephone. Ask
yourself: *If I knew I wasn't going to get a comment on this post, would I still
post it?* If the answer is no, step away from the keyboard.

▶ **Address the real issue.** If you're stressed out, anxious, or have relationship issues, get help for the real problem rather than burying yourself
online.

▶ **Identify triggers.** Are you bored or lonely? If so, create a list of alter-
nate ways of dealing with those feelings.

▶ **Reduce time spent online.** Total abstinence is unlikely given the
extreme usefulness of the Internet, so set reasonable goals instead.
For example, if you spend ten hours a day online, cut back by two
hours. Write in your calendar when you'll allow time to use. Plan
short but regular use as this will help to eliminate cravings and withdrawal symptoms.

▶ **Rearrange your schedule to disrupt your routine.** If you typically
check e-mail first thing in the morning, wait until after breakfast. If you
usually go online immediately after work, do it after dinner.

▶ **Disrupt the pattern of your behavior by doing things you'd
normally do online in real life.** For example, replace sending online
greeting cards with actual cards from the store.

Advice for
Exercise Addicts:

▶ **Examine your motives.** Ask yourself, *What am I running from?*
Work on underlying issues of depression, anxiety, self-confidence, and
body image.

▶ **Change your thinking.** More isn't necessarily better. Work out
smarter.

▶ **Have fun and exercise in group settings.** This reduces your drive
toward perfection.

▶ **Hire a trainer.** Work with a fitness professional who can help you
develop a healthy exercise routine and realistic goals.

▶ **Balance the rest of your life too.** Make sure you are not channeling
your exercise addiction into your work, family life, or somewhere else.

▶ **Develop a life outside of the gym.** In your free time do something
unrelated to fitness, such as see movies, read, or hang out with friends.

Acknowledgments

Behind every dream and every goal is a team of supporters. My supporters included family, friends, colleagues, and various editors and agents. They were always there for me. They believed in me, and they were devoted to seeing this project through. Without them, *Be Fearless* would be nothing more than an idea.

Thank you to my editor at Center Street, Kate Hartson, for her hard work under tight time constraints. Many thanks to the rest of the Center Street team, including Rolf Zettersten, publisher; Bob Castillo, senior production editor; Harry Helm, associate publisher; Andrea Glickson, marketing director; publicists Jessica Zimmerman and Sarah Reck; and the entire sales team.

One fateful day in March 2010, I was on TV talking about infidelity, and so was an author who had just written a book about marriage. Little did I know that day would change my life. That author turned out to be Alisa Bowman, a *New York Times* bestselling writer. We talked about her book and my approach to therapy. I quickly realized that Alisa was one of those rare people who genuinely care. We exchanged numbers, and she later took the time to offer me some advice on how to go about writing a book.

A few months later, much to my delight, she came to me and said she'd like to work with me. I was thrilled to have such an esteemed collaborator on my project. Her expertise, nurturing, support, and many pep talks make her a truly gifted collaborator who knows how to make a great idea shine on paper. Alisa, you've worn many hats, not the least of which is that of friend. Thank you for believing in me when my ideas were merely a concept and for your patience every step of the way.

To my literary agent, Wendy Sherman, a seasoned professional who tirelessly worked to make dozens of things fall into place and to make this book a reality. Thank you for taking me on as a client and holding my hand throughout this often arduous and anxiety-provoking process. You have quite a knack for calming my worries and clearing the path for me to achieve a dream.

To agent Michael Harriot, from Folio Literary. Thank you for offering your invaluable support and opinions on so many things that came up throughout the process and for believing in me and entrusting your fearless writer Alisa Bowman to me.

Thank you to agent Jenny Meyer, for securing so many book deals around the world.

Thank you to Ann-Marie Nieves at Get Red PR for your expertise.

To my wise friend John Lane, who has always managed to find the positive in a situation, even when I didn't always see it. Thank you for your fine editing of my various writings and for continuing to explain to me the proper use of *I* and *me*.

To JoAnn Kim, who has been an unwavering source of support. You're always there to listen, help me solve problems, and generally make my struggles feel less burdensome. Thank you for the countless words you've written and edited on my behalf. I am lucky to have you as a friend.

To my sister, Susan Scala. Thank you for your enthusiasm for the book, your support, and for taking the time to provide your help and opinion on titles and head shots. What you say truly matters.

To my brother, Matthew Alpert. I am forever grateful for your steady support and for always listening to me, even when I talked nonsense. Thank you for your continued selflessness and generosity, especially when times were less good. I couldn't ask for a better brother or friend.

To my mother, Sheila Alpert, and my late father, Joseph Alpert. You've shown me just how compassionate people can be. Even during your most difficult times, you found a way to help others. Your love for each other and for the family is truly remarkable. I am thankful for your support and for all the sacrifices you've made for the family. Without you, my dreams and goals would have remained impossible. Your encouragement, belief in me, and ability to keep me level headed are invaluable. Thank you for hanging on over the years through the many dramas and crises. Even in the midst of your own stress, you always found a way to make mine a little less intense. Sometimes it was merely hearing your voice that made all the difference in the world. I am superproud of this book, but that pales in comparison to how proud I am to have you as my parents.

Mom, our frequent chats remind me of how lucky I am to have a mother who cares as much as you do. Your compassion and ability to understand others always impresses me, and you truly are the therapist in the family. You have definitely helped to make me the person and therapist that I am today.

Dad, I'll never forget your calming voice of reason. You are always with me in spirit, reminding me to take one step at a time and helping me through whatever challenges I may face. Throughout your life, you served as a living example of how to face challenges with optimism. You've made me a better man and a better person and taught me so much about life that I will never forget. I miss you dearly.

To the countless clients I've helped over the years: Thank you for your confidence and trust in my abilities. Your successes never cease to delight me, and you truly capture the essence of the BE FEARLESS program. Thank you also to those clients who lent their stories to me for the sake of this book. Your amazing tales found on these pages have inspired me and will surely inspire readers.

JONATHAN ALPERT is a psychotherapist, columnist, and executive coach in Manhattan. He has helped countless clients overcome a wide range of challenges and achieve success. He discussed his results-oriented approach in his 2012 *New York Times* Opinion piece, "In Therapy Forever? Enough Already," which continues to be debated and garner international attention. Alpert is frequently interviewed by major TV, print, radio, and digital media outlets, and he has appeared on the *Today Show*, CNN, FOX, and *Good Morning America* to discuss current events, mental health, hard news stories, and celebrities/politicians, as well as lifestyle and hot-button issues. He also appears in the 2010 Oscar-winning documentary *Inside Job* and has been a spokesperson for major brands including Enterprise Rent-A-Car, Liberty Mutual Insurance, and NutriBullet. Alpert penned the popular "No More Drama" column for *Metro* newspapers from 2006 to 2013 and continues to provide advice to the masses through his *Inc.com* and *Thrive Global* columns.

Follow him on Twitter at @JonathanAlpert and learn more at jonathanalpert.com.

Writer ALISA BOWMAN has been the collaborator on seven *New York Times* bestsellers, and her books have sold over two million copies.